Rust System Programming

Build Secure, Concurrent, and Efficient System Software

Jose Gobert

Copyright Page

Table of Contents

Preface

Systems programming is the foundation of every operating system, runtime, embedded device, and network stack you rely on daily. It's the kind of programming that interacts closely with the machine, manages memory manually, handles concurrency, and runs under strict performance and safety constraints. For decades, this kind of work was the exclusive domain of C and C++. These languages provided the raw access developers needed but came with significant trade-offs in safety, maintainability, and long-term reliability. Today, Rust offers a modern and safer path for building the same kinds of powerful, efficient, low-level software—without losing control or introducing runtime overhead.

Why Rust for Systems Programming

Rust was designed from the beginning to enable reliable and efficient systems software development. Its core features—ownership, borrowing, and lifetimes—make it possible to write memory-safe code without a garbage collector. That means your programs can run with performance on par with C, but without the memory leaks, null pointer dereferencing, and use-after-free bugs that have haunted systems programming for years.

Rust's compile-time checks enforce strict memory safety rules, which drastically reduces the chances of bugs that can lead to crashes or vulnerabilities. These checks are not optional—they're built into the way you write code. Once your program compiles, you gain a strong level of assurance that it behaves safely with respect to memory.

Concurrency is another area where Rust shines. Writing multithreaded code has always been difficult, especially when trying to avoid race conditions, data corruption, or deadlocks. Rust's type system helps catch concurrency issues at compile time, preventing many of the bugs that traditionally only show up at runtime in other languages. This is not just convenient—it's transformational. It allows you to build scalable, high-performance software without fearing the pitfalls of shared state and parallel execution.

The modern tooling ecosystem also makes Rust a practical choice. Cargo, Rust's package manager and build system, simplifies everything from project scaffolding to dependency management and unit testing. The language has a rapidly growing library ecosystem and is supported by an active community that values correctness, clarity, and transparency.

Who This Book is For

This book is written for developers who want to build fast, secure, and reliable system-level software using a modern programming language. If you're coming from a C or C++ background, you'll find Rust offers you similar control over performance and memory, but with far better safety guarantees and more expressive tools.

If you're a high-level developer—perhaps working in Python, Java, or JavaScript—and you've wanted to understand how the systems below your applications really work, Rust is a great language to grow into. It may feel unfamiliar at first, but this book is designed to explain every concept clearly, connect it to real problems, and provide working examples to reinforce your understanding.

This book will also appeal to embedded developers, systems engineers, backend developers interested in low-level optimizations, or anyone interested in secure, concurrent software. You do not need prior Rust experience, but you should be comfortable reading and writing code, understanding how computers manage memory, and working with basic command-line tools.

What You'll Learn and Build

Throughout this book, you'll learn how to write Rust code that interacts directly with system resources—files, memory, threads, devices, and networks. You'll gain a solid understanding of how Rust manages ownership and lifetimes to prevent common bugs, and how to write concurrent programs that are fast and safe. You'll also learn how to use Rust's powerful type system and ecosystem tools to design efficient, testable, and maintainable systems code.

Beyond learning, you'll build. Each chapter is grounded in real-world use cases. You'll develop foundational systems components like a memory allocator, a multithreaded task runner, a TCP server, and tools that interact with the operating system or run on bare-metal environments. You'll see how to connect to C libraries, manage memory without a garbage collector, and even write software for embedded devices.

By the end of this book, you won't just understand how Rust works—you'll be able to confidently use it to create reliable, high-performance systems that are maintainable and secure. The goal is not just to teach you syntax, but to show you how to think like a systems programmer using Rust's tools and mindset.

This is systems programming, reimagined with safety and modern language design. Whether you're starting from scratch or refining your skills, this book will equip you to write code that's fast, fearless, and fit for production.

Chapter 1: Systems Programming with Rust

Writing software that interacts directly with hardware, manages memory explicitly, or handles thousands of concurrent requests is very different from building a web page or a mobile app. Systems programming is about giving software precise control over performance and resource usage. It's about writing the kind of code that powers kernels, embedded firmware, compilers, device drivers, low-level networking tools, and high-performance services. And it's exactly the kind of code that Rust was designed to make safer, more reliable, and easier to maintain.

Let's start by grounding ourselves in what systems programming actually is, then look at how Rust fits into the picture—and why it's different from everything that came before it.

Understanding the Role of Systems Programming

Systems programming is the kind of programming that builds the software infrastructure every other application runs on. When you think about what makes your operating system boot, what controls your network card, how files are read from disk, or how an embedded sensor communicates with the rest of the hardware, that's systems programming in action. It's about writing software that directly manages hardware, memory, and the low-level services that power everything else. But to really understand systems programming, we need to talk about what makes it fundamentally different from application development.

When you build web applications or mobile apps, you're usually working with high-level frameworks. These frameworks abstract away details like how memory is allocated, how threads are managed, or how system calls reach the kernel. You write logic in terms of models, views, APIs, or user events. Performance is still important, but you're usually buffered by layers of abstraction that manage resources for you—often through runtime engines or garbage collectors.

Systems programming strips all of that away. It hands you the bare metal, so to speak, and asks you to be responsible for everything. You allocate memory manually. You decide when to free it. You control how threads interact and how concurrency is managed. You determine when to access disk or send network packets, and you do it through system calls or memory-mapped I/O.

Let's put this in a real-world context. Suppose you're writing a simple TCP server that handles requests from clients over a network socket. In a high-level language like Python or JavaScript, this might involve calling a library function like `socket.listen()` or using an HTTP framework that hides most of the networking details. You rarely deal with socket descriptors, memory buffers, or manual threading.

But in a systems language, you're directly interfacing with the operating system. You open sockets using file descriptors. You control whether data is read in blocking or non-blocking mode. You decide whether to spin up threads manually, use a thread pool, or handle connections asynchronously. And if a connection is dropped or memory is leaked, your program is the one to crash—or worse, to corrupt the system it's running on.

Here's a basic example to illustrate this in Rust. The code below shows how you'd write a low-level TCP listener in Rust that handles each incoming connection in a new thread. This is very much a systems programming task:

```rust
use std::net::{TcpListener, TcpStream};
use std::io::{Read, Write};
use std::thread;

fn handle_client(mut stream: TcpStream) {
    let mut buffer = [0; 512];
    match stream.read(&mut buffer) {
        Ok(size) => {
            println!("Received: {}",
String::from_utf8_lossy(&buffer[..size]));
            let _ = stream.write(b"HTTP/1.1 200
OK\r\n\r\nHello from Rust!\n");
        }
        Err(e) => {
            eprintln!("Failed to read from
connection: {}", e);
        }
```

```
        }
}

fn main() -> std::io::Result<()> {
    let listener =
TcpListener::bind("127.0.0.1:7878")?;

    for stream in listener.incoming() {
        match stream {
            Ok(stream) => {
                thread::spawn(||
handle_client(stream));
            }
            Err(e) => {
                eprintln!("Failed to accept
connection: {}", e);
            }
        }
    }

    Ok(())
}
```

This code doesn't rely on a web framework. It binds to a TCP port, waits for connections, and spawns a new thread for each client. You're seeing the core pieces of systems programming: file descriptors, byte buffers, threading, and error handling. It's your job to make sure that every open connection is properly closed, that memory isn't leaked, and that threads don't overwhelm the system under high load.

But systems programming is not limited to networking. The same principles apply whether you're writing a custom allocator, building an operating system kernel, interfacing with sensors in an embedded device, or writing a compiler backend that translates code to machine instructions. In all of these areas, you're working in an environment where there's little room for error and even less for inefficiency.

That brings in the idea of determinism. In systems programming, the predictability of how resources are used is critical. You want to know when memory is allocated and deallocated. You want to ensure that critical sections of code are thread-safe without relying on chance. You want to be able to reason about the performance of every line of code—because performance isn't a bonus, it's a requirement.

This is also why traditional systems languages like C are so widely used despite their age. They offer a high degree of control. You can write to memory addresses directly. You can control how data is aligned in memory or how fast a tight loop runs. But with that control comes danger. A single unchecked pointer can corrupt memory. An off-by-one error in an array can crash the kernel. A forgotten `free()` call can leak memory and degrade performance over time.

Rust addresses these challenges not by limiting what you can do, but by enforcing rules about how you do it. You still have full control, but you have to work within a system of guarantees. If your code compiles, it's not just syntactically correct—it also respects ownership, borrowing rules, and memory safety guarantees. That's why Rust is often described as empowering: it lets you write the same kind of low-level, high-performance code that systems programming requires, but without having to write your own tooling to catch common errors.

One of the most important things to understand about systems programming is that it's everywhere. It's not just something done by operating system developers. It underlies your database engine, your embedded smart devices, your streaming platform, and the firmware that runs inside your keyboard. Every high-level system is built on top of layers of systems software. And those layers need to be fast, secure, and stable.

So when you choose to learn systems programming with Rust, you're not just learning a language. You're learning how to build the software foundation that everything else depends on. You're learning how to manage memory precisely, how to handle concurrency responsibly, and how to make software that performs predictably and safely even under the most demanding conditions.

How Rust Changes the Landscape

To understand how Rust transforms systems programming, you have to start with a clear understanding of the problems it was created to solve. For decades, developers have relied on C and C++ for low-level programming because those languages give you full control over memory, processor instructions, and direct hardware access. But that control comes at a steep cost. You're responsible for manually managing memory, synchronizing threads, and avoiding undefined behavior. If you make a mistake—and everyone eventually does—it often shows up as a memory leak, segmentation fault, data race, or worse, a security vulnerability that can be exploited in production.

Rust changes that equation by giving you the same low-level power, but with a compiler that enforces strict safety rules at compile time. Instead of pushing all responsibility to you as the programmer, Rust shares the burden by embedding correctness directly into the language design. It's not just syntactic sugar over C—it's a rethink of how systems programming should be done in a modern, multi-core, security-conscious world.

At the center of Rust's innovation is its ownership model. Every value in Rust has a single owner, and when that owner goes out of scope, the value is automatically cleaned up. This sounds simple, but the implications are profound. It means memory is automatically reclaimed without needing a garbage collector. It also means that the compiler can detect if you're trying to use memory after it's been freed—a common and dangerous bug in C and C++.

Let's take a quick look at what ownership looks like in practice:

```
fn main() {
    let data = String::from("hello");
    let other = data; // Ownership is moved here

    // println!("{}", data); // This will not
compile
    println!("{}", other);
}
```

In this code, the variable `data` owns a `String`. When we assign `data` to `other`, ownership is moved—`data` is no longer valid. If you try to use `data` after this point, the compiler will raise an error. This might seem restrictive at first, but it's actually what protects your code from accessing freed memory.

In C or C++, this scenario could lead to a use-after-free bug, which is notoriously difficult to detect and often exploited for malicious purposes. Rust prevents this entirely at compile time.

Now let's go a bit further. Suppose you want to write a function that takes a reference to a value without taking ownership of it. Rust makes you be explicit about lifetimes and borrowing, which protects you from dangling references:

```
fn greet(name: &str) {
    println!("Hello, {}", name);
}

fn main() {
    let name = String::from("Alice");
    greet(&name); // Borrowing, not moving
ownership
    println!("Still valid: {}", name);
}
```

Here, greet borrows a reference to name, but name still owns the data. After the function call, name can still be used because its ownership never changed. The compiler tracks this relationship and guarantees safety across the lifetime of the reference.

This strict tracking of ownership and borrowing enables you to write code that is **both safe and fast**. There's no garbage collector pausing execution. There's no reference counting unless you explicitly choose it. And you never have to worry about invalid memory access—because it's not just discouraged, it's disallowed by the compiler.

Now let's talk about concurrency—another area where Rust completely changes the rules. In C and C++, writing thread-safe code is hard. It's easy to create race conditions, deadlocks, or access data from multiple threads in ways that result in unpredictable behavior. Rust prevents data races at compile time using the same ownership model. If a value is being accessed mutably by one thread, no other thread can access it at the same time unless it's explicitly synchronized.

Here's a basic example using threads and message passing:

```
use std::thread;
```

```
use std::sync::mpsc;

fn main() {
    let (sender, receiver) = mpsc::channel();

    let handle = thread::spawn(move || {
        sender.send("Hello from the
thread").unwrap();
    });

    let message = receiver.recv().unwrap();
    println!("{}", message);

    handle.join().unwrap();
}
```

In this example, we create a thread that sends a message back to the main thread using a channel. Because we're using `move`, the sender is transferred into the thread safely. The compiler ensures that ownership rules are respected and that no two threads are accessing the same data in an unsafe way. This is a huge improvement over traditional languages where concurrency issues often only appear at runtime and are extremely hard to debug.

Rust also provides low-level tools like `Mutex`, `RwLock`, `Atomic` types, and thread-safe smart pointers such as `Arc` (atomic reference counting). These are essential for sharing data safely between threads. And the best part? The compiler ensures that these constructs are used safely. You can't forget to lock a mutex or accidentally access a value without synchronization—the compiler will reject unsafe patterns before they run.

Another way Rust changes the landscape is through its ecosystem and tooling. Rust includes a tool called Cargo, which handles everything from compiling your code to managing dependencies, running tests, and building release binaries. It enforces project structure, provides built-in support for documentation, and even lets you publish libraries to the official registry, crates.io.

This means you're not just learning a language—you're adopting a complete, integrated toolchain that is consistent, fast, and built with developer productivity in mind. In contrast, systems languages like C often rely on a fragmented ecosystem of build systems, makefiles, and compiler flags. Rust gives you a single, unified experience that works out of the box.

Lastly, Rust's error messages are some of the most informative you'll ever see. When something goes wrong, the compiler doesn't just say "you did something wrong." It tells you exactly what the problem is, where it occurred, and what you can do to fix it. This is particularly valuable when learning concepts like lifetimes, which can be difficult to grasp initially.

The end result is that you can build powerful systems software—TCP servers, file systems, device drivers, embedded firmware—with confidence that your code is not only fast, but safe, reliable, and easier to maintain than anything you'd write in C or C++.

Rust doesn't just improve how we write systems code. It redefines the standard of what we should expect from systems programming languages. It offers safety without sacrificing control, modern tools without overhead, and concurrency that's not just possible—but encouraged and safe. These aren't surface-level features. They go right to the core of how your software behaves—and that's what makes Rust a game changer for systems development.

Performance, Safety, and Control

In systems programming, performance, safety, and control are all non-negotiable. But in most traditional languages, you're usually forced to choose two out of the three. You can have performance and control with C, but you sacrifice safety. You can have safety and decent ergonomics with a language like Java or Go, but you lose fine-grained control and raw speed. Rust is different. It's designed from the ground up to give you all three at once—and it enforces that promise through strict rules, zero-cost abstractions, and compile-time guarantees that catch bugs before they can reach production.

When we talk about **performance**, we're referring to how fast your software runs and how efficiently it uses system resources—CPU, memory, I/O, and bandwidth. In Rust, performance is a first-class concern. The compiler aggressively optimizes your code, generating machine instructions that are on par with or even faster than equivalent C code in many cases. There's no garbage collector pausing your threads. No dynamic runtime dispatch unless you explicitly ask for it. Every abstraction in Rust is either zero-cost or opt-in. That means the abstractions you use in your source code don't add overhead unless you deliberately introduce it.

Take this basic example of summing numbers using a for-loop and iterators:

```
fn sum_loop() -> i32 {
    let mut total = 0;
    for i in 0..1_000_000 {
        total += i;
    }
    total
}

fn sum_iterator() -> i32 {
    (0..1_000_000).sum()
}
```

Both functions achieve the same result—summing numbers from 0 to 999,999. Even though `sum_iterator` uses a functional, higher-level style, Rust's compiler optimizes it into the same machine code as the more manual loop. This is what zero-cost abstraction means: the elegant version doesn't make your program slower. The abstractions are removed entirely at compile time, leaving behind code that is as efficient as handwritten loops in C.

That's performance, but what about **safety**?

Rust is unmatched in the level of safety it brings to systems programming. This safety is built directly into the type system and enforced at compile time. Common memory bugs—use-after-free, null pointer dereferencing, buffer overflows—are simply not possible in safe Rust. The ownership model, combined with strict borrowing and lifetime rules, ensures that memory access is always valid and race-free. If you try to break those rules, your code won't compile.

Here's an example of Rust preventing a use-after-free error:

```
fn use_after_free() {
    let s = String::from("hello");
    let r = &s;
    drop(s); // Explicitly drop the original value
```

```
    // println!("{}", r); // Compiler error: borrow
after move
}
```

In this snippet, the compiler prevents you from using `r` after the original `String` has been dropped. In C, you'd have no such guard—`r` would now be pointing to freed memory, and using it would result in undefined behavior. In Rust, the compiler enforces correct behavior before the code even runs. That's not just safe—it's predictable and dependable.

Now, you might be wondering how Rust handles **control**. After all, control in systems programming means more than just choosing data types. It means being able to manage memory manually, define your own allocators, write inline assembly, interact directly with hardware registers, or link against system libraries.

Rust doesn't take control away from you. In fact, it gives you more control—but it does so responsibly. Unsafe code is still allowed in Rust, but it's isolated and explicit. You have to mark sections of your code as `unsafe`, and you become solely responsible for upholding Rust's safety guarantees within those sections. The compiler still checks everything outside of them.

Here's a small but illustrative example using raw pointers and unsafe code:

```
fn unsafe_memory_access() {
    let x = 42;
    let r = &x as *const i32;

    unsafe {
        println!("Value at pointer: {}", *r);
    }
}
```

This function reads the value of a raw pointer. This is not allowed in safe Rust, but you can do it in an `unsafe` block. You're telling the compiler: "I know what I'm doing here." This model keeps the power and control in your hands, but also helps you isolate and audit unsafe sections of your code when needed.

Let's now consider a real-world scenario where performance, safety, and control matter—writing a custom memory allocator. In Rust, you can override the default allocator and provide your own logic for allocating and freeing

17

memory. You might do this for embedded systems where memory layout needs to be deterministic, or in performance-critical applications where every byte counts.

Here's a simplified example of a global allocator using a bump allocator:

```rust
use std::alloc::{GlobalAlloc, Layout};
use std::ptr::null_mut;
use std::sync::Mutex;

struct BumpAllocator {
    heap_start: usize,
    heap_end: usize,
    next: usize,
}

unsafe impl GlobalAlloc for BumpAllocator {
    unsafe fn alloc(&self, layout: Layout) -> *mut u8 {
        let size = layout.size();
        let align = layout.align();

        let alloc_start = (self.next + align - 1) & !(align - 1);
        let alloc_end = alloc_start + size;

        if alloc_end > self.heap_end {
            null_mut()
        } else {
            self.next = alloc_end;
            alloc_start as *mut u8
        }
    }

    unsafe fn dealloc(&self, _ptr: *mut u8, _layout: Layout) {
        // No deallocation in a bump allocator
    }
}
```

This example uses unsafe Rust because you're directly manipulating raw memory, bypassing Rust's usual ownership checks. But it's still safer than

18

equivalent C code, because the rest of your program remains safe and protected by the compiler's checks. You're allowed to take full control when needed—but only when you make it explicit.

That's the key idea here: **Rust gives you the full power of systems programming but wraps it in guardrails that prevent catastrophic mistakes unless you choose to step outside them.** You get the kind of fine-grained control you'd expect in C, the performance you need for embedded or high-performance workloads, and a type system that ensures your code is free of memory and concurrency errors—before it runs.

There's no trade-off here. You don't have to give up safety to get speed. You don't have to give up control to get productivity. You don't have to wait for runtime exceptions to tell you something went wrong. Rust brings a new model to systems programming: one that treats safety and performance not as opposing goals, but as qualities that reinforce each other through disciplined language design.

Chapter 2: Core Rust for Systems Development

Before you can write efficient, safe, and low-level systems software in Rust, you need to master three foundational concepts: ownership, borrowing, and lifetimes. These are the pillars of Rust's memory safety model, and they enable you to write systems-level code without worrying about undefined behavior or manual memory cleanup.

This chapter will walk you through what these concepts are, how they work under the hood, and why they matter so much in a systems programming context. We'll also get into raw pointers, low-level data types, and introduce you to `unsafe` Rust—how it works, when it's necessary, and how to use it responsibly without undermining the guarantees the rest of the language provides.

Ownership, Borrowing, and Lifetimes

When working in Rust—especially in systems programming—you don't just write code to get things done. You write code to control memory, to ensure stability under pressure, and to eliminate undefined behavior before it can take root. To do this well, you need to understand three of Rust's most important concepts: ownership, borrowing, and lifetimes. These are not surface-level syntactic sugar. They are structural features of the language that provide memory safety without requiring a garbage collector or runtime engine.

If you've used languages like C or C++, then you're already familiar with the responsibilities of memory management: allocating, using, and freeing memory. But those languages don't check whether memory is used safely. You can read from freed memory. You can write past the end of an array. And you can forget to free memory entirely, leading to leaks.

Rust enforces strict discipline at compile time to prevent those issues, and it does this through ownership.

How Ownership Works in Rust

In Rust, **every piece of memory is owned by a single variable**. That owner is responsible for cleaning it up. When the owner goes out of scope, the memory is automatically freed. No function calls are needed—no `free()`, no garbage collector, and no tracing at runtime. The compiler tracks everything statically.

Let's go through a simple example:

```
fn main() {
    let s = String::from("hello");
    println!("{}", s); // OK
} // `s` is dropped here, memory is freed
automatically
```

In this code, the `String` object is allocated on the heap. When `s` goes out of scope at the end of `main`, the memory it used is automatically released. This is predictable and deterministic.

But what happens when you try to assign that value to another variable?

```
fn main() {
    let a = String::from("Rust");
    let b = a;

    println!("{}", b); // OK
    // println!("{}", a); // X Error: `a` was
moved
}
```

When `b = a` runs, ownership of the `String` is **moved** from a to b. After this, a is no longer valid. If you try to use a, the compiler will catch it as an error.

Why does this matter? Because it avoids the classic bugs you'd find in C where two pointers reference the same memory and one of them frees it, leaving the other pointing to garbage. In Rust, once a value moves, the original owner is no longer allowed to use it.

This single-owner principle is a foundation of memory safety in Rust. And while it may feel restrictive at first, it prevents a wide class of errors that are extremely hard to catch in other systems languages.

Understanding Borrowing

Sometimes you don't want to give up ownership—you just want to **let someone else temporarily read or modify the value you own**. That's called **borrowing**, and Rust allows it in two flavors: immutable and mutable borrowing.

Here's immutable borrowing:

```
fn print_message(msg: &String) {
    println!("{}", msg);
}

fn main() {
    let greeting = String::from("Hi from Rust");
    print_message(&greeting); // Borrowing
    println!("Still valid: {}", greeting); // OK
}
```

By passing `&greeting`, you're telling the compiler: "Let `print_message` use this, but don't let it change it, and I still own it afterward." That's an immutable borrow.

Now let's look at mutable borrowing:

```
fn add_exclamation(text: &mut String) {
    text.push_str("!");
}

fn main() {
    let mut message = String::from("Wow");
    add_exclamation(&mut message);
    println!("{}", message); // Prints: Wow!
}
```

With `&mut`, you allow a function to change your value—but only **one mutable borrow is allowed at a time**. You can't have multiple mutable references, and you can't mix mutable and immutable references. This is how Rust prevents race conditions at the data level.

For example, this won't compile:

```
fn main() {
    let mut s = String::from("safe");
```

```
    let r1 = &s;
    let r2 = &s;

    let r3 = &mut s; // X Error: cannot borrow as
mutable while borrowed as immutable

    println!("{}, {}", r1, r2);
}
```

This rule may seem strict, but it enforces a principle that has long been elusive in systems programming: **aliasing and mutation cannot happen at the same time**. This removes entire classes of concurrency bugs.

Why Lifetimes Matter

Ownership and borrowing work together to give you static guarantees about memory safety. But sometimes, Rust needs help understanding how long references are valid. That's where **lifetimes** come in.

A **lifetime** is the scope during which a reference is valid. Rust uses lifetimes to make sure that references never outlive the data they point to.

Let's consider this example:

```
fn longest(x: &str, y: &str) -> &str {
    if x.len() > y.len() {
        x
    } else {
        y
    }
}
```

This will raise a compiler error, because Rust doesn't know whether the returned reference will live as long as both x and y. You fix this by using explicit lifetime annotations:

```
fn longest<'a>(x: &'a str, y: &'a str) -> &'a str {
    if x.len() > y.len() {
        x
    } else {
        y
    }
}
```

23

Here, 'a is a lifetime parameter that tells the compiler: "The returned reference will be valid as long as both inputs are valid for the same lifetime 'a." This allows Rust to guarantee that the reference will never outlive the data it refers to.

Let's break that down with a practical use case.

Suppose you're building a string search utility that returns a reference to the first match in a large dataset. That function should not create a new string—it should return a reference to the original data for performance reasons. But you need to guarantee that the data will still be around when the reference is used.

```
fn find_match<'a>(text: &'a str, pattern: &str) ->
Option<&'a str> {
    text.find(pattern).map(|i| &text[i..i +
pattern.len()])
}
```

This function searches for a pattern in the given text and returns a reference to the match. Because of the lifetime 'a, the compiler knows that the returned reference is only valid as long as text is valid. This prevents you from accidentally storing the result in a longer-lived variable than the original text itself.

Exercises for Practical Understanding

Let's practice a few concepts to solidify your understanding.

Exercise 1: Ownership Transfer

```
fn main() {
    let original = String::from("ownership");
    let moved = original;

    // Try uncommenting the line below. What
happens?
    // println!("{}", original);
}
```

Task: Understand why the compiler prevents you from using original after the move.

Exercise 2: Multiple Borrows

```
fn main() {
    let mut val = String::from("Rust");

    let r1 = &val;
    let r2 = &val;
    println!("{}, {}", r1, r2);

    // Uncomment the next line. What happens and
why?
    // let r3 = &mut val;
}
```

Task: Observe the compile error and reflect on how Rust protects you from race conditions.

Exercise 3: Lifetime Fix

```
fn return_ref(x: &str, y: &str) -> &str {
    if x.len() > y.len() {
        x
    } else {
        y
    }
}
```

Task: Add the appropriate lifetime annotation to make the function compile.

Understanding ownership, borrowing, and lifetimes gives you the confidence to write code that is safe and correct—even when you're operating close to the hardware. These features are not limitations—they are tools of precision. They make your intentions clear, your data flow explicit, and your systems software robust.

You no longer need to worry about who frees memory, whether a reference is dangling, or if a thread will corrupt shared state. Rust checks all of this at compile time and gives you the control back—on your terms, and with clarity.

In the next section, you'll start applying these concepts to build low-level systems features like memory management, file access, and concurrency—all in a way that respects Rust's guarantees while giving you full control over your system's behavior.

Low-Level Data Types and Pointers

When you're building systems software, you often have to work close to the hardware—reading from raw memory, manipulating binary data structures, interfacing with device registers, or building your own memory allocators. At this level, every byte counts. Every memory access has to be precise. And that's where low-level data types and pointers come in. In C or C++, these are your bread and butter—but they come with a lot of risk. Rust gives you these same tools but surrounds them with a language design that forces discipline and clarity.

Working with Primitive Data Types

Rust gives you a full suite of primitive types that map directly to how data is stored in memory. These are fixed-size types, with no surprises:

```
let a: u8 = 255;       // 8-bit unsigned

let b: i16 = -32768; // 16-bit signed

let c: u32 = 1000;     // 32-bit unsigned

let d: i64 = -1;       // 64-bit signed

let f: f32 = 3.14;     // 32-bit float

let g: bool = true;

let h: char = 'R';
```

These types behave exactly as their names suggest. There's no ambiguity about how many bits are used or what the memory representation is. This is critical when you're communicating across a hardware bus, writing to a network socket, or designing a binary file format.

Rust also supports compound types like tuples and arrays, but when performance and layout matter, you'll often want to define your own structures using `struct`.

Structs and Memory Layout

A `struct` in Rust is a collection of fields grouped together. When you define a struct, you're essentially defining how a chunk of memory is organized.

```
struct Point {
    x: i32,
    y: i32,
}

fn main() {
    let p = Point { x: 10, y: 20 };
    println!("({}, {})", p.x, p.y);
}
```

This is simple, but behind the scenes, Rust is laying out `Point` in memory as 8 bytes: 4 for `x` and 4 for `y`. But this layout is not guaranteed unless you specify it.

When interfacing with C code or hardware registers, you need to ensure that Rust lays out your structures exactly as you expect. For that, you use `#[repr(C)]`:

```
#[repr(C)]
struct Header {
    magic: u16,
    version: u16,
    flags: u32,
}
```

This tells the compiler: use C-compatible layout rules. That means fields are laid out in order, with predictable padding and alignment. This is essential when building parsers for binary protocols, talking to firmware, or accessing memory-mapped device registers.

Using Raw Pointers Safely

Now let's get into pointers.

Rust has two kinds of safe references: `&T` and `&mut T`. These are tracked by the borrow checker, and they're safe by design. But sometimes you need to go lower—especially when interfacing with external systems or manipulating memory directly. That's where **raw pointers** come in: `*const T` and `*mut T`.

These behave like C pointers. They can point to anything—including invalid or freed memory. Because of that, raw pointers are **unsafe**. You can create them in safe code, but you can only dereference them inside an `unsafe` block.

Here's an example:

```
fn main() {
    let x = 123;
    let ptr = &x as *const i32;

    unsafe {
        println!("Pointer points to: {}", *ptr);
    }
}
```

The pointer `ptr` holds the address of `x`. We convert a safe reference `&x` to a raw pointer `*const i32`. Then, in the `unsafe` block, we dereference it to read the value. This is one of the simplest examples of using raw pointers, and it works because we know `x` is valid.

But what happens when you deal with pointers that come from external sources—say, a hardware buffer or a system API? You must check that the pointer is valid, aligned, and properly typed. Rust gives you the power, but not the permission, to do unsafe things by accident.

Mutating Memory with Raw Pointers

If you want to **write** to memory through a pointer, you use `*mut T`:

```
fn main() {
    let mut value = 10;
    let ptr = &mut value as *mut i32;

    unsafe {
        *ptr = 42;
    }

    println!("Updated value: {}", value); // 42
}
```

Again, this works only in an `unsafe` block. The compiler trusts that you've ensured safety.

Pointer Arithmetic and Offsets

In some cases, you may need to walk through memory manually—just like pointer arithmetic in C. Rust allows this, but it's up to you to make sure you're not reading garbage memory.

Here's a practical example:

```
fn main() {
    let arr = [10, 20, 30, 40];
    let ptr = arr.as_ptr();

    unsafe {
        println!("{}", *ptr.offset(2)); // 30
    }
}
```

We get a raw pointer to the first element of the array using `.as_ptr()`, then read the third element by applying an offset of 2. Again, you're responsible for bounds checking. Rust will not stop you from walking off the end of the array if you misuse this.

This kind of logic is common when writing allocators, buffer parsers, or device drivers.

Real-World Example: Memory-Mapped I/O

Let's say you're working on an embedded system, and you need to access a peripheral device through a memory-mapped register at a specific address. You'd do something like this:

```
#[repr(C)]
struct GpioRegister {
    ctrl: u32,
    status: u32,
}

const GPIO_BASE: usize = 0x4000_0000;

fn main() {
    let gpio = GPIO_BASE as *mut GpioRegister;

    unsafe {
```

```
        (*gpio).ctrl = 0b0001_0000;
        let status = (*gpio).status;
        println!("GPIO status: {:#X}", status);
    }
}
```

Here, we cast the address 0x4000_0000 into a raw pointer to a GpioRegister struct. Then, using unsafe dereferencing, we write to the control register and read from the status register.

This is standard in embedded systems and systems programming, and Rust handles it cleanly—forcing you to isolate unsafe operations and leaving the rest of your code safe and trackable.

Practical Exercise

Here's something you can try to reinforce your understanding.

Exercise: Build a Struct and Access It via Pointer

```
#[repr(C)]
struct Pixel {
    r: u8,
    g: u8,
    b: u8,
    a: u8,
}

fn main() {
    let pixel = Pixel { r: 255, g: 127, b: 64, a:
255 };

    let ptr = &pixel as *const Pixel;

    unsafe {
        println!("Red: {}", (*ptr).r);
        println!("Green: {}", (*ptr).g);
        println!("Blue: {}", (*ptr).b);
        println!("Alpha: {}", (*ptr).a);
    }
}
```

Task: Modify the struct fields using *mut Pixel and observe the effect.

When you understand how to work with raw pointers, low-level types, and memory layout in Rust, you can write systems code that is both expressive and powerful. Whether you're building a custom allocator, parsing a binary protocol, or accessing hardware, Rust lets you do it with precision—and in most cases, with better safety than legacy languages allow.

The next section will introduce you to `unsafe` Rust—how to use it responsibly, when it's unavoidable, and how to isolate it so the rest of your codebase stays reliable and maintainable.

Unsafe Rust

Most of the time, Rust protects you from yourself. It ensures you can't dereference invalid memory, access data out of bounds, create data races, or leave use-after-free bugs lurking in your code. But there are moments in systems programming where you need to do things the compiler can't fully verify—like talking to hardware registers, calling foreign code, managing memory manually, or working with uninitialized buffers for performance. These are the places where safe Rust stops, and `unsafe` Rust begins.

Now, calling something "unsafe" doesn't mean it's wrong or dangerous by default. It means you're stepping outside the automatic safety guarantees, and **you** become responsible for upholding the rules the compiler normally enforces. If you're precise and understand what you're doing, unsafe code can be perfectly correct and even necessary. But if you're careless, you open the door to the kinds of bugs Rust was designed to prevent.

What Does `unsafe` Mean in Rust?

The `unsafe` keyword gives you access to capabilities that are blocked in safe Rust. These include:

Dereferencing raw pointers

Calling functions or methods marked as `unsafe`

Accessing or modifying mutable static variables

Accessing union fields

Invoking inline assembly

Here's the simplest example:

```
fn main() {
    let x = 5;
    let r = &x as *const i32;

    unsafe {
        println!("Value: {}", *r);
    }
}
```

In this code, we convert a safe reference `&x` into a raw pointer `*const i32`, and then we dereference it inside an `unsafe` block. The compiler won't check whether `r` points to valid memory. That's your job. You've told the compiler, "I know this is okay, trust me."

And if you're wrong—if the pointer was invalid or came from a corrupt source—you can cause undefined behavior, which might lead to crashes, data corruption, or security vulnerabilities.

This is why unsafe code should be isolated, small, and well-audited. You don't make an entire module unsafe—you make **only the lines that need to be**.

When Should You Use Unsafe Rust?

Unsafe Rust is typically used in low-level systems tasks. Here are some legitimate use cases that often require it:

Interfacing with C code (FFI):
You may need to call functions from the C standard library, interact with system APIs, or link with hardware-specific routines provided in C.

```
extern "C" {
    fn abs(input: i32) -> i32;
}

fn main() {
    unsafe {
        println!("abs(-3): {}", abs(-3));
    }
}
```

You're calling a foreign function defined in another language, so Rust can't verify its behavior. The `unsafe` block marks that boundary clearly.

Manual memory management:

If you're implementing a memory pool or allocator, you might allocate memory using raw pointers and manually construct or deconstruct values.

```
use std::alloc::{alloc, dealloc, Layout};

fn main() {
    unsafe {
        let layout = Layout::new::<u64>();
        let ptr = alloc(layout) as *mut u64;

        if !ptr.is_null() {
            *ptr = 0xABCD_EFFF;
            println!("Allocated value: {:#X}",
*ptr);
            dealloc(ptr as *mut u8, layout);
        }
    }
}
```

This kind of code is common in systems programming. It gives you full control, but it also demands precision. If you forget to free memory or write to a null pointer, Rust can't save you.

Interacting with hardware or memory-mapped I/O:

You might need to write values to specific addresses in memory that represent device registers.

```
const REGISTER: *mut u32 = 0x4000_0000 as *mut u32;

fn write_to_register(value: u32) {
    unsafe {
        *REGISTER = value;
    }
}
```

The compiler can't verify whether `0x4000_0000` is a valid address. That's your responsibility, based on hardware documentation. This is standard practice in embedded development.

Implementing synchronization primitives:

If you're building a low-level `Mutex`, atomic queue, or spinlock, you might need to use raw pointers and data structures that temporarily break borrowing rules.

In these cases, Rust gives you the tools—but also asks you to prove your understanding. It gives you nothing for free.

Best Practices for Using Unsafe Code

Just because you *can* use unsafe doesn't mean you *should*—at least not without care. There's a disciplined way to write unsafe code that protects your overall system. Here are a few rules of thumb:

Minimize the scope of unsafety.

Only mark the lines or blocks that require unsafe operations. Don't wrap whole functions or modules in `unsafe` unless every part of them truly requires it.

```
unsafe {
    // One line that needs to be unsafe
    *ptr = 42;
}
```

Wrap unsafe code in safe abstractions.

Your goal should be to use unsafe code to build safe APIs. Once you've tested and verified the unsafe logic, expose a safe interface to the rest of your application.

For example:

```
fn write_raw(ptr: *mut u32, value: u32) {
    unsafe {
        if !ptr.is_null() {
            *ptr = value;
        }
    }
}
```

Callers never touch unsafe blocks, even though they're using a pointer behind the scenes.

Document your assumptions.

Unsafe code always comes with assumptions. Is the pointer aligned? Is it non-null? Is the memory initialized? Is it not shared? Document those assumptions clearly in comments above the unsafe block. That way, you— and anyone maintaining the code later—understand what conditions must hold for the code to be correct.

Test and audit thoroughly.

Unsafe code needs more scrutiny. Write tests. Use sanitizers. Use tools like miri to detect undefined behavior. Don't treat unsafe like normal code—it's not. It deserves more care.

Real-World Example: Creating an Uninitialized Buffer

Suppose you want to build a fast byte buffer for receiving network data. To avoid initializing memory unnecessarily, you use an uninitialized buffer:

```
use std::mem::MaybeUninit;

fn main() {
    let mut buf: [MaybeUninit<u8>; 1024] = unsafe {
        MaybeUninit::uninit().assume_init()
    };

    // Safe initialization
    for i in 0..1024 {
        buf[i] = MaybeUninit::new(i as u8);
    }

    // Convert to a fully-initialized buffer
    let initialized: [u8; 1024] = unsafe {
        std::mem::transmute_copy(&buf)
    };

    println!("First byte: {}", initialized[0]);
}
```

This is advanced Rust, but it shows how unsafe code lets you avoid unnecessary initialization for performance reasons. You assume the risk, but you do it in a way that's controlled and intentional.

35

Unsafe Rust is not a fallback or a dirty trick. It's part of the language, and it exists for good reason. In systems programming, there are tasks that simply can't be done safely because the compiler doesn't have enough information. You still need the power of direct memory access, foreign function calls, and low-level bit manipulation.

Rust doesn't take that power away—it just puts a clear label on it and demands that you step up to use it properly.

If you respect the boundaries, isolate your unsafe code, and wrap it in safe, tested abstractions, you can build the same kinds of high-performance systems as you would in C or C++—but with a fraction of the risk and a significantly higher level of confidence in your code's behavior.

Chapter 3: Memory Management

When you're writing systems-level code, memory isn't just something you use—it's something you manage. You don't get automatic cleanup. You don't have a garbage collector running in the background. And you can't afford to leak memory or accidentally overwrite something that should still be in use. Rust was designed specifically to help you handle memory precisely and safely—without a garbage collector, and without the manual headache that C and C++ developers are used to.

In this chapter, you'll learn how Rust gives you fine-grained control over memory, while still ensuring safety through strict compile-time checks. We'll start with understanding how memory is organized (stack vs heap), then explore how Rust helps you manage heap allocation with smart pointers like `Box`, `Rc`, and `Arc`. Finally, we'll look at how to enable controlled mutability in otherwise immutable contexts through interior mutability patterns like `RefCell` and `Cell`.

Heap and Stack Allocation

In systems programming, how you manage memory isn't just a performance concern—it's often a matter of correctness and reliability. Understanding the difference between **stack** and **heap** allocation is one of the most fundamental things you can learn when writing low-level software in Rust. These two memory regions behave very differently, and using them appropriately can mean the difference between fast, deterministic code and slow, unpredictable execution.

What is Stack Allocation?

The **stack** is a region of memory where values are stored in a very specific way: last-in, first-out. When a function is called, a new **stack frame** is pushed onto the stack. This frame contains function arguments, local variables, and bookkeeping information. When the function exits, the frame is popped off the stack. This process is fast and extremely predictable because the memory is released automatically—there's no cleanup function to call, and no allocator is involved.

Rust places simple, fixed-size values on the stack whenever possible. These include integers, booleans, characters, and fixed-size structs. Because stack memory is automatically cleaned up at the end of a function's execution, you don't have to explicitly deallocate anything.

Let's look at a simple example:

```
fn print_values() {
    let a = 10;
    let b = 20;
    println!("a + b = {}", a + b);
}

fn main() {
    print_values();
}
```

Here, `a` and `b` are both stored on the stack. As soon as `print_values()` returns, the memory for `a` and `b` is automatically released. There's no manual deallocation. This is efficient because the stack doesn't need to search for free space—allocation is just a pointer bump, and deallocation is implicit when the function returns.

Stack-allocated memory is also **cache-friendly** due to its locality. Because most modern processors use CPU caches to speed up memory access, placing small data tightly together on the stack can give a real performance boost.

What is Heap Allocation?

The **heap**, by contrast, is a region of memory used for **dynamic** allocation. You use it when you don't know how much memory you'll need at compile time, or when you need memory to live beyond the function that creates it. Allocating on the heap is more flexible—but it comes with a cost.

Heap allocation is **slower** than stack allocation. You have to ask the allocator to find a block of free memory large enough to hold your data. It also doesn't automatically deallocate when the function ends—you have to track and clean it up yourself, or rely on the language to do so. In Rust, this cleanup is handled through ownership and automatic memory management via the type system.

In Rust, the primary way to allocate memory on the heap is with the `Box` type:

```
fn main() {
    let x = Box::new(42);
    println!("Boxed value: {}", x);
}
```

Here, x is a pointer to memory on the heap that stores the value 42. The pointer itself is stored on the stack, but the integer is on the heap. When x goes out of scope, Rust drops the Box and automatically frees the heap memory—safely and deterministically.

Heap allocation is especially useful for large data structures or for values that need to be shared or mutated across function boundaries, or in cases where values grow in size at runtime (like vectors or strings).

For example, this is how you'd dynamically allocate a list of integers:

```
fn main() {
    let numbers = vec![1, 2, 3, 4, 5];
    println!("{:?}", numbers);
}
```

The vector's contents live on the heap, but the Vec itself (which stores a pointer, capacity, and length) lives on the stack.

When to Use Stack vs Heap

Use the stack when:

The size of your data is known at compile time

You don't need to return data beyond the scope of the current function

Performance and predictability are critical

The data is small and doesn't need to be resized or shared

Use the heap when:

You need to allocate a value at runtime

You need the value to live beyond the current stack frame

The size or structure of your data might change dynamically

You're passing large or shared data between functions, threads, or data structures

Let's look at a practical scenario. Suppose you're implementing a tree structure in Rust. You can't use simple stack allocation because each node potentially owns children, and the size of the entire structure is not known at compile time. You'll need heap allocation.

```rust
use std::boxed::Box;

struct Node {
    value: i32,
    left: Option<Box<Node>>,
    right: Option<Box<Node>>,
}

fn main() {
    let tree = Node {
        value: 10,
        left: Some(Box::new(Node {
            value: 5,
            left: None,
            right: None,
        })),
        right: Some(Box::new(Node {
            value: 15,
            left: None,
            right: None,
        })),
    };

    println!("Root value: {}", tree.value);
}
```

Each `Node` is stored on the heap, and the `Box` ensures the memory is cleaned up when the owning variable is dropped.

Exercise: Visualize Stack vs Heap

Here's a helpful way to internalize the behavior. Try stepping through the following code with `cargo run --release` and inspect what's happening:

```rust
fn create_boxed_value() -> Box<i32> {
```

```
    let x = Box::new(123);
    x
}

fn main() {
    let stack_val = 456;
    let heap_val = create_boxed_value();

    println!("Stack value: {}", stack_val);
    println!("Heap value: {}", heap_val);
}
```

Task: Explain where each value is stored and what happens to that memory when `main()` ends. How does Rust handle the cleanup?

Why This Matters in Systems Programming

In systems development, understanding where your data lives and how long it lives is critical. You might be writing performance-sensitive code like network servers, memory allocators, task schedulers, or even OS kernels. The ability to distinguish between stack and heap memory, and the ability to choose the right kind for the job, affects everything from speed to reliability.

More importantly, Rust's strict enforcement of memory ownership, lifetime, and borrowing rules ensures that stack and heap memory are both used **correctly**. You never allocate memory and forget to free it. You never free something twice. And you never access memory after it's been released.

This safety comes without a garbage collector, without runtime checks (unless you explicitly ask for them), and with no hidden costs. Rust gives you the power of C, but with protection where it matters.

In the next section, we'll explore how to manage heap-allocated data more flexibly—using smart pointers like `Box`, `Rc`, and `Arc` to model ownership, sharing, and mutation in ways that are safe, ergonomic, and ideal for systems-level software.

Manual Resource Management with Box, Rc, and Arc

In traditional systems programming, when you allocate memory manually, you're also responsible for freeing it. If you forget, you leak memory. If you free it twice, you get undefined behavior. And if you use it after freeing it, the program may crash—or worse, corrupt data silently. This burden has made memory bugs some of the most painful and expensive issues to deal with in C and C++.

Rust changes that equation completely, but without giving up manual control. The language doesn't use a garbage collector. Instead, it uses the concept of **ownership** and powerful smart pointer types like Box, Rc, and Arc to track memory at compile time. These tools let you manage heap-allocated memory predictably, safely, and without runtime overhead—unless you explicitly ask for it.

Owning Heap Memory with Box

The Box<T> type is the simplest way to allocate a value on the heap. When you create a Box, it stores your data in heap memory, but ownership of that memory remains tied to the Box itself. When the Box goes out of scope, its memory is automatically and safely freed.

Here's a concrete example:

```
fn main() {
    let x = Box::new(42);
    println!("Boxed value: {}", x);
}
```

This is heap allocation under your control—but with none of the risks of malloc and free. The value 42 is stored in heap memory, and x is the owner. You can't clone a Box<T> by default because it's designed to represent exclusive ownership. If you want to move the value elsewhere, you can, but you lose the original reference:

```
fn main() {
    let a = Box::new(100);
    let b = a; // ownership moves here
```

```
    // println!("{}", a); // ✗ This would cause a
compile error
    println!("{}", b); // ☑ OK
}
```

This behavior ensures there's never any ambiguity about who's responsible for the memory.

A great use case for Box is recursive data structures. Since Rust requires that types have a known size at compile time, recursion can be tricky unless you box the recursive elements.

Here's an example of a simple linked list:

```
enum List {
    Cons(i32, Box<List>),
    Nil,
}

fn main() {
    let list = List::Cons(1, Box::new(List::Cons(2,
Box::new(List::Nil))));
}
```

Each Cons variant owns a Box<List>, which allows the list to grow dynamically while maintaining memory safety.

Shared Ownership with Rc

Sometimes, you need **multiple parts of your program** to share ownership of a value. This is common in data structures like graphs or trees with shared branches. Box can't help you here—it enforces exclusive ownership. That's where Rc<T> comes in.

Rc stands for **Reference Counted**. It allows multiple owners of the same heap-allocated data in a **single-threaded** context. It keeps a count of how many Rc instances point to the same data. When the count reaches zero, the memory is freed.

Let's walk through a practical example:

```rust
use std::rc::Rc;

fn main() {
    let data = Rc::new(String::from("shared"));

    let a = Rc::clone(&data);
    let b = Rc::clone(&data);

    println!("a: {}", a);
    println!("b: {}", b);
    println!("Reference count: {}",
Rc::strong_count(&data));
}
```

Here, the `String` is heap-allocated once, but shared between `data`, `a`, and `b`. Cloning an `Rc` doesn't copy the data—it just increments the reference count. Rust manages the count automatically and deallocates the memory only when the last owner goes out of scope.

This is useful for building **shared, acyclic data structures** where multiple parts of a program need read access to the same object without duplicating memory.

But `Rc` only works in single-threaded programs. If you try to send an `Rc` across threads, Rust will stop you with a compile-time error. That brings us to `Arc`.

Thread-Safe Shared Ownership with `Arc`

When you need to share ownership **between threads**, you use `Arc<T>`—short for **Atomic Reference Counted**. It behaves like `Rc`, but it uses atomic operations to safely update the reference count across threads. This makes it slightly slower than `Rc`, but it's thread-safe and necessary for concurrency.

Here's an example that uses `Arc` with multiple threads:

```rust
use std::sync::Arc;
use std::thread;

fn main() {
    let message = Arc::new(String::from("Hello from
threads!"));
```

44

```
    let mut handles = vec![];

    for _ in 0..4 {
        let msg_clone = Arc::clone(&message);
        let handle = thread::spawn(move || {
            println!("{}", msg_clone);
        });
        handles.push(handle);
    }

    for handle in handles {
        handle.join().unwrap();
    }
}
```

Each thread receives a clone of the Arc, and all threads share the same underlying String. The reference count is updated atomically, ensuring safe memory access even under concurrent conditions.

Note that Arc<T> only provides **shared read access**. If you need **mutability**, you'll have to pair it with a synchronization primitive like Mutex<T>. Here's how that would look:

```
use std::sync::{Arc, Mutex};
use std::thread;

fn main() {
    let counter = Arc::new(Mutex::new(0));
    let mut handles = vec![];

    for _ in 0..5 {
        let counter_clone = Arc::clone(&counter);
        let handle = thread::spawn(move || {
            let mut num =
counter_clone.lock().unwrap();
            *num += 1;
        });
        handles.push(handle);
    }

    for handle in handles {
        handle.join().unwrap();
```

```
    }

    println!("Final count: {}",
*counter.lock().unwrap());
}
```

In this case, `Arc` allows shared ownership between threads, and `Mutex` provides safe, exclusive access to the internal data.

Exercise: Practice Manual Memory Management

Try this exercise to strengthen your understanding:

```
use std::rc::Rc;

struct Person {
    name: String,
}

fn main() {
    let alice = Rc::new(Person { name:
String::from("Alice") });

    let friend1 = Rc::clone(&alice);
    let friend2 = Rc::clone(&alice);

    println!("{} has {} friends", alice.name,
Rc::strong_count(&alice) - 1);
}
```

Task: Modify the code to add more friends, and watch how the reference count changes. Then, let some clones go out of scope and see when the object is deallocated.

When working with low-level memory in systems programming, you don't want guesswork. You want precision. Rust gives you that through `Box`, `Rc`, and `Arc`:

`Box` gives you exclusive heap ownership, ideal for tree-like structures or large objects.

`Rc` enables multiple ownership in single-threaded programs, useful for shared graphs or model-view-controller patterns.

`Arc` gives you the same power in concurrent programs, with safe reference counting across threads.

In every case, Rust's type system and ownership model make memory safety a **compile-time guarantee**, not a runtime gamble. You get the power to manage memory manually—but without the mistakes that make traditional systems programming so error-prone.

Interior Mutability and Smart Pointers

Rust encourages immutability by default. When you define a variable as `let x = 5`, it's not just a convention—it's a strict rule. You can't change `x` unless you explicitly declare it mutable. The same applies to references. If you borrow something as immutable, the compiler guarantees that it won't be changed through that reference.

This behavior enforces a strong and clear separation between reading and writing, which is one of the pillars of Rust's safety guarantees. But there are times when that model becomes too rigid—especially when working with shared data in layered abstractions, closures, or reference-counted pointers like `Rc`.

That's where **interior mutability** comes in. Rust provides types that allow you to mutate data even through an immutable reference, as long as you follow certain rules that are enforced either at runtime or through special APIs. This gives you controlled escape hatches that preserve the overall safety model while enabling patterns that wouldn't be possible otherwise.

In this section, we'll explore how interior mutability works in practice through three powerful tools: `Cell`, `RefCell`, and `Mutex`—each serving slightly different use cases depending on whether your code is single-threaded or multithreaded.

Mutating Copy Types with `Cell`

Let's start with the simplest: `Cell<T>`. This type is designed to enable interior mutability for **copy types**—values like integers, booleans, and other types that implement the `Copy` trait.

With `Cell`, you can store a value, read it, and update it—even if the `Cell` itself is behind an immutable reference.

```
use std::cell::Cell;

fn main() {
    let data = Cell::new(10);

    println!("Initial value: {}", data.get());

    data.set(42);
    println!("Updated value: {}", data.get());
}
```

This is legal even though `data` is not marked as mutable. The trick is that `Cell` works by **copying values in and out** rather than giving out references. You can't get a reference to the inner value, but you can replace it or fetch a copy.

This is particularly useful in scenarios like caching flags or counters inside an immutable struct:

```
struct Counter {
    count: Cell<u32>,
}

impl Counter {
    fn increment(&self) {
        self.count.set(self.count.get() + 1);
    }

    fn get(&self) -> u32 {
        self.count.get()
    }
}

fn main() {
    let counter = Counter { count: Cell::new(0) };

    counter.increment();
    counter.increment();

    println!("Count: {}", counter.get()); //
Output: Count: 2
```

```
}
```

You're able to mutate the internal value even though the `Counter` instance itself is immutable. This is safe because `u32` implements `Copy` and `Cell` doesn't expose shared references.

Borrow-Checked Mutability with `RefCell`

When you need interior mutability for non-`Copy` types—like `String`, `Vec`, or custom structs—you use `RefCell<T>`. This type allows borrowing mutable or immutable references at runtime, rather than compile time.

```
use std::cell::RefCell;

fn main() {
    let text = RefCell::new(String::from("Hello"));

    text.borrow_mut().push_str(", Rust!");

    println!("Updated text: {}", text.borrow());
}
```

Here's the important distinction: `RefCell` enforces borrowing **rules at runtime**, not compile time. That means you can do things like borrow mutably from an immutable reference, but if you break the rules—say, try to borrow mutably while another borrow is still active—it panics.

Let's look at what happens when you make an invalid access:

```
fn main() {
    let data = RefCell::new(vec![1, 2, 3]);

    let borrow1 = data.borrow();
    let borrow2 = data.borrow(); // ✓ OK: two
shared borrows
    println!("{:?}, {:?}", borrow1, borrow2);

    let borrow_mut = data.borrow_mut(); // ✗
Panics: cannot borrow mutably while immutably
borrowed
    println!("{:?}", borrow_mut);
}
```

49

Rust will compile this code, but panic at runtime when it detects a mutable borrow while immutable borrows are still in scope.

You typically use `RefCell` in conjunction with `Rc` when building data structures where multiple owners need to mutate the same data. Here's a more complex, but realistic example:

```rust
use std::cell::RefCell;
use std::rc::Rc;

struct Node {
    value: i32,
    next: Option<Rc<RefCell<Node>>>,
}

fn main() {
    let node1 = Rc::new(RefCell::new(Node { value: 1, next: None }));
    let node2 = Rc::new(RefCell::new(Node { value: 2, next: Some(Rc::clone(&node1)) }));

    // Mutate node1 through shared Rc<RefCell<Node>>
    node1.borrow_mut().value = 10;

    println!("Node1 value: {}", node1.borrow().value);
}
```

This pattern—`Rc<RefCell<T>>`—is one of the most common ways to build flexible, tree-like, or graph-like structures in Rust where ownership is shared, and mutation is allowed.

Thread-Safe Interior Mutability with `Mutex`

If you're working in a multithreaded context, `RefCell` won't cut it. It's not thread-safe. For those situations, Rust offers types like `Mutex<T>` and `RwLock<T>`, which enable interior mutability **across threads** using locks.

Here's how you can use `Mutex`:

```rust
use std::sync::{Arc, Mutex};
```

```
use std::thread;

fn main() {
    let data = Arc::new(Mutex::new(0));
    let mut handles = vec![];

    for _ in 0..4 {
        let data_cloned = Arc::clone(&data);
        let handle = thread::spawn(move || {
            let mut value =
data_cloned.lock().unwrap();
            *value += 1;
        });
        handles.push(handle);
    }

    for handle in handles {
        handle.join().unwrap();
    }

    println!("Final value: {}",
*data.lock().unwrap());
}
```

In this example, we combine `Arc` for shared ownership and `Mutex` for interior mutability across threads. Each thread locks the mutex, modifies the value, and then unlocks it automatically when the `MutexGuard` is dropped.

This is how you achieve **safe concurrent mutation** in Rust—without sacrificing the guarantees that make the language trustworthy.

Exercise: Use `RefCell` in Shared Context

```
use std::cell::RefCell;
use std::rc::Rc;

fn main() {
    let shared_vec = Rc::new(RefCell::new(vec![1,
2, 3]));

    {
        let mut vec_ref = shared_vec.borrow_mut();
        vec_ref.push(4);
```

```
        vec_ref.push(5);
    }

    println!("Shared vector: {:?}",
shared_vec.borrow());
}
```

Task: Add more logic to sort or remove elements from the vector. Observe how RefCell allows mutable access in a shared, owned context.

When Should You Use Each?

Use Cell<T> for simple Copy types that don't require references.

Use RefCell<T> for complex types when you need interior mutability in single-threaded code.

Use Mutex<T> or RwLock<T> for data shared and mutated across threads.

Combine Rc with RefCell, or Arc with Mutex, depending on your thread-safety needs.

Each of these types enables powerful memory and data-sharing patterns that would otherwise require unsafe code in C or C++. Rust wraps them in clear rules and expressive APIs, allowing you to control when and how mutability occurs—without breaking the guarantees that make your systems software reliable.

Interior mutability isn't a workaround—it's a core capability in Rust's systems programming toolkit. Use it wisely, document your assumptions, and always keep safety front and center.

Chapter 4: Concurrency

Concurrency has always been one of the most difficult areas in systems programming. Getting it right means your software can do more work in less time, scale across multiple CPU cores, and respond to events without blocking. Getting it wrong can lead to elusive bugs, unpredictable crashes, corrupted memory, or deadlocks that freeze entire systems.

What makes concurrency difficult is that multiple threads or processes often need to work with shared data. In traditional systems languages like C or C++, managing concurrent access is entirely up to the developer—with no help from the compiler. It's shockingly easy to introduce a race condition or access memory unsafely when several threads are reading and writing simultaneously.

Rust offers a radically safer model. It gives you full power to write low-level concurrent code, but it combines that with strong compile-time rules that eliminate common concurrency bugs before they happen. In this chapter, we'll look at how Rust handles concurrency through threads, channels, atomic types, and synchronization primitives like mutexes and locks—without making you trade away performance or control.

Threads, Channels, and Message Passing

In systems programming, concurrency is about getting more done at once—without waiting on slow tasks or blocking the rest of your system. Whether you're writing a server that handles hundreds of simultaneous requests or a program that offloads expensive work to background workers, you'll eventually need threads. But just spawning threads isn't enough—you need a way for them to coordinate. That's where message passing comes in.

Rust gives you a clean and safe way to do both. You can spawn threads with `std::thread`, and you can pass data between them using channels from `std::sync::mpsc`. The best part is that all of this is checked by the compiler. No shared mutable state, no data races, no surprises. You write your code, and Rust ensures the communication is correct, or it won't compile.

Spawning Threads

Creating a thread in Rust is straightforward. You use the `thread::spawn` function and pass it a closure. This closure is what the thread will run.

```
use std::thread;

fn main() {
    let handle = thread::spawn(|| {
        for i in 1..=5 {
            println!("From thread: {}", i);
        }
    });

    for i in 1..=5 {
        println!("From main: {}", i);
    }

    handle.join().unwrap();
}
```

Here's what's happening:

The `spawn` function starts a new thread immediately.

The closure passed to `spawn` runs in that new thread.

The `join()` call waits for the thread to finish.

Without `join()`, the main thread could finish before the spawned thread completes. Always join if your program needs to wait for threads to finish before exiting.

If you need to move data into a thread, you must use the `move` keyword to transfer ownership into the closure:

```
use std::thread;

fn main() {
    let message = String::from("Hello from
thread");

    let handle = thread::spawn(move || {
        println!("{}", message);
    });
```

```
    handle.join().unwrap();
}
```

Rust won't allow you to reference a variable from another thread unless ownership is moved, because references across threads could cause data races. This restriction protects you from undefined behavior.

Channels: Safe Communication Between Threads

Creating threads is easy. The harder part is getting them to talk to each other. Rust solves this with **channels**.

A channel has two endpoints:

A **sender** (tx)

A **receiver** (rx)

You send data through the sender, and receive it from the receiver.

Here's the simplest example:

```
use std::sync::mpsc;
use std::thread;

fn main() {
    let (tx, rx) = mpsc::channel();

    thread::spawn(move || {
        let data = String::from("Hello from
worker");
        tx.send(data).unwrap();
    });

    let received = rx.recv().unwrap();
    println!("Main thread received: {}", received);
}
```

The call to `mpsc::channel()` returns a transmitter and a receiver. The transmitter is sent into the thread using `move`. Then, `tx.send(data)` sends the message, and `rx.recv()` blocks the main thread until it receives something.

This is **message passing** in action. There's no shared memory here—just ownership being transferred safely from one thread to another.

If you want to send multiple messages, the channel stays open until the sender is dropped. You can loop over rx like this:

```
use std::sync::mpsc;
use std::thread;
use std::time::Duration;

fn main() {
    let (tx, rx) = mpsc::channel();

    thread::spawn(move || {
        let messages = vec!["starting", "in
progress", "almost done", "done"];
        for msg in messages {
            tx.send(msg).unwrap();

thread::sleep(Duration::from_millis(300));
        }
    });

    for received in rx {
        println!("Main got: {}", received);
    }
}
```

Once the thread finishes and the tx is dropped, the loop over rx ends naturally. This makes channels ideal for streaming data from producers to consumers.

Cloning Senders for Multiple Producers

In some designs, you'll have multiple threads producing messages and one thread consuming them. Rust's Sender can be cloned, which allows multiple producers to use the same channel:

```
use std::sync::mpsc;
use std::thread;

fn main() {
    let (tx, rx) = mpsc::channel();
```

```
    for i in 0..3 {
        let tx_clone = tx.clone();
        thread::spawn(move || {
            let msg = format!("Message from thread
{}", i);
            tx_clone.send(msg).unwrap();
        });
    }

    for _ in 0..3 {
        let received = rx.recv().unwrap();
        println!("Main received: {}", received);
    }
}
```

Each thread gets its own copy of the transmitter. They all send messages to the same receiver. This pattern works great for job dispatching, logging, or collecting results.

Note that `Sender` is the only part you can clone. You cannot clone the `Receiver`, because the channel must have a single reader to ensure consistency and prevent race conditions.

Exercises for Practice

Try building a simple task queue with multiple producers and one consumer.

```
use std::sync::mpsc;
use std::thread;

fn main() {
    let (tx, rx) = mpsc::channel();

    for i in 0..5 {
        let tx_clone = tx.clone();
        thread::spawn(move || {
            let job = format!("Task {}", i);
            tx_clone.send(job).unwrap();
        });
    }

    drop(tx); // Important: Drop the original
sender to close the channel
```

57

```
for received in rx {
    println!("Processing {}", received);
}
}
```

Challenge: Extend this by using `std::sync::Arc` and `Mutex` to add shared state—like a completed task counter or shared output buffer.

Rust encourages message passing because it avoids the hardest problems of concurrency: shared mutable state. Instead of fighting the borrow checker to allow multiple threads to mutate data, you pass ownership from one thread to another. No locks, no deadlocks, no data races.

This makes your code simpler to write, easier to reason about, and safer to maintain. In real-world systems—whether you're building a network service, simulation engine, or compiler backend—this model lets you build scalable, predictable concurrency without giving up the control that systems programming demands.

Mutexes, Atomics, and Locks

When you're building systems software that runs in multiple threads, you're eventually going to run into a situation where data has to be shared. You can't always pass ownership around like you do with channels. Sometimes, several threads need to look at the same data—and maybe even modify it. That's where things get tricky.

In most languages, shared memory in concurrent programs is a dangerous space. If two threads try to write to the same location at the same time—or one tries to read while the other writes—you get race conditions. These bugs are hard to find, hard to test, and can break your system in unpredictable ways.

Rust handles this differently. It gives you tools like `Mutex`, `RwLock`, and atomic types such as `AtomicUsize`—but with type system restrictions and compile-time rules that make misuse much harder. You still get the control you need, but in a way that forces you to be precise and safe.

Sharing Data Across Threads with `Mutex`

58

The `Mutex<T>` type allows multiple threads to safely share access to a single value. At any moment, only one thread can lock the mutex and access the value inside. This ensures **mutual exclusion**, meaning no two threads can use the data at the same time.

Here's a simple example:

```rust
use std::sync::{Arc, Mutex};
use std::thread;

fn main() {
    let counter = Arc::new(Mutex::new(0));

    let mut handles = vec![];

    for _ in 0..5 {
        let counter_clone = Arc::clone(&counter);
        let handle = thread::spawn(move || {
            let mut num =
counter_clone.lock().unwrap();
            *num += 1;
        });
        handles.push(handle);
    }

    for handle in handles {
        handle.join().unwrap();
    }

    println!("Final count: {}",
*counter.lock().unwrap());
}
```

Here's how this works:

`Arc<T>` (Atomic Reference Counted) allows the `counter` to be shared between threads.

`Mutex<T>` wraps the integer so that only one thread can modify it at a time.

`.lock().unwrap()` locks the mutex and gives you a `MutexGuard`, which automatically releases the lock when it goes out of scope.

This model guarantees that no two threads can increment the counter at the same time. If one thread is holding the lock, all others are blocked until the lock is released.

It's important to call `.unwrap()` after `.lock()` because the lock can fail (e.g., if the mutex is poisoned by a panic in another thread). In production code, you may want to handle this more gracefully.

Locking Patterns and Pitfalls

A `Mutex` works by blocking the current thread until it can safely access the data. That's powerful, but it also opens the door to **deadlocks**—when two or more threads are waiting on each other forever.

Here's a classic case of deadlock:

```rust
use std::sync::{Arc, Mutex};
use std::thread;

fn main() {
    let a = Arc::new(Mutex::new(1));
    let b = Arc::new(Mutex::new(2));

    let a1 = Arc::clone(&a);
    let b1 = Arc::clone(&b);
    let t1 = thread::spawn(move || {
        let _a_lock = a1.lock().unwrap();
        let _b_lock = b1.lock().unwrap();
        println!("Thread 1: locked a then b");
    });

    let a2 = Arc::clone(&a);
    let b2 = Arc::clone(&b);
    let t2 = thread::spawn(move || {
        let _b_lock = b2.lock().unwrap();
        let _a_lock = a2.lock().unwrap();
        println!("Thread 2: locked b then a");
    });

    t1.join().unwrap();
    t2.join().unwrap();
}
```

Each thread locks one mutex and then tries to lock another. If both threads get the first lock before the other releases the second, the program freezes. To avoid this, **always lock multiple resources in a consistent order across all threads**.

Atomic Types for Lock-Free Data

Sometimes, all you need is a simple counter or flag—something small and fast, where locking might be overkill. Rust's atomic types give you **lock-free synchronization** for primitive data types.

Let's look at `AtomicUsize`:

```
use std::sync::atomic::{AtomicUsize, Ordering};
use std::thread;

fn main() {
    let counter = AtomicUsize::new(0);

    let mut handles = vec![];

    for _ in 0..5 {
        let counter_ref = &counter;
        let handle = thread::spawn(move || {
            counter_ref.fetch_add(1,
Ordering::SeqCst);
        });
        handles.push(handle);
    }

    for handle in handles {
        handle.join().unwrap();
    }

    println!("Atomic counter: {}",
counter.load(Ordering::SeqCst));
}
```

This is an efficient and safe way to increment a counter from multiple threads. It uses atomic CPU instructions under the hood, so there's no mutex, no lock contention, and no risk of data races.

But it's not magic. Atomic operations require you to specify memory **ordering**—rules about how the CPU and compiler can reorder instructions. The most conservative is `Ordering::SeqCst` (sequentially consistent), which preserves the strictest semantics and is safest to start with.

If you're writing high-performance systems code like schedulers or allocators, atomics are indispensable. They allow you to build lock-free data structures with fine-tuned control over performance and visibility.

Exercise: Shared Log Buffer with Mutex

Try building a shared buffer that collects log messages from multiple threads.

```rust
use std::sync::{Arc, Mutex};
use std::thread;

fn main() {
    let log = Arc::new(Mutex::new(Vec::new()));

    let mut handles = vec![];

    for i in 0..4 {
        let log_clone = Arc::clone(&log);
        let handle = thread::spawn(move || {
            let mut buffer =
log_clone.lock().unwrap();
            buffer.push(format!("Thread {} logged
this", i));
        });
        handles.push(handle);
    }

    for handle in handles {
        handle.join().unwrap();
    }

    println!("Log contents:");
    for entry in log.lock().unwrap().iter() {
        println!("{}", entry);
    }
}
```

Challenge: Extend this to sort the log or write it to disk.

When to Use Mutexes vs Atomics

Use a `Mutex` when:

You need to protect a complex data structure.

You want to mutate data shared between threads.

You don't need extremely low-latency access.

Use atomic types when:

You're updating a primitive (like a flag or counter).

You care about minimal overhead.

You understand memory ordering and are building low-level lock-free structures.

Both are tools for synchronization—but they solve different kinds of problems.

In a language like Rust, concurrency is not just possible—it's structured, predictable, and safe. You don't have to guess whether your shared data is protected. The compiler will guide you. You don't have to hope you remembered to release a lock. RAII ensures it happens automatically.

`Mutex`, `Arc`, and atomic types give you full control over synchronization without the risks of C-style manual memory management. The result is software that scales with modern CPUs, behaves correctly under load, and is maintainable over time.

In the next section, we'll take what you've learned here and focus on concurrency correctness—avoiding race conditions, preventing deadlocks, and reasoning clearly about thread interaction in systems code.

Avoiding Race Conditions and Deadlocks

Concurrency can make software faster, more responsive, and better at scaling—but it can also introduce some of the most subtle and damaging bugs in systems programming. Two of the most serious issues you'll face when writing multithreaded programs are **race conditions** and **deadlocks**. These problems don't always show up during testing. Sometimes they appear under rare timing conditions, or only on certain hardware, making them extremely hard to reproduce or detect without careful design.

A **race condition** occurs when two or more threads access the same memory at the same time, and at least one of them writes to it. The program's behavior then depends on the unpredictable timing of the threads, which leads to nondeterministic bugs. These are dangerous because they can corrupt data silently, crash your system, or create subtle inconsistencies that go unnoticed until something breaks.

Let's look at a simplified version of what a race condition might look like (in a language that allows it):

```
int counter = 0;
```

```
// Thread A
counter += 1;
```

```
// Thread B
counter += 1;
```

This may look harmless, but the `+= 1` operation is not atomic. It involves reading the value, incrementing it, and writing it back. If two threads read at the same time, both might write back the same result, effectively losing one increment.

In Rust, this kind of unsynchronized access is not allowed. The compiler will prevent you from compiling code that allows multiple threads to access mutable data without synchronization.

Let's do it the correct way using a `Mutex`:

```
use std::sync::{Arc, Mutex};
use std::thread;
```

```
fn main() {
    let counter = Arc::new(Mutex::new(0));
    let mut handles = vec![];

    for _ in 0..10 {
        let counter = Arc::clone(&counter);
        let handle = thread::spawn(move || {
            let mut num = counter.lock().unwrap();
            *num += 1;
        });
        handles.push(handle);
    }

    for handle in handles {
        handle.join().unwrap();
    }

    println!("Final count: {}",
*counter.lock().unwrap());
}
```

Here, we use:

Arc to allow multiple threads to share ownership of the Mutex.

Mutex to ensure that only one thread can modify the counter at a time.

A scoped MutexGuard that automatically unlocks when the thread is done.

Because all access to the shared counter is protected, there's no race condition.

You can also use atomic types for smaller data, such as AtomicUsize:

```
use std::sync::atomic::{AtomicUsize, Ordering};
use std::thread;

fn main() {
    let counter = AtomicUsize::new(0);
    let mut handles = vec![];

    for _ in 0..10 {
        let handle = thread::spawn({
            let counter_ref = &counter;
            move || {
```

```
                    counter_ref.fetch_add(1,
Ordering::SeqCst);
                }
        });
        handles.push(handle);
    }

    for handle in handles {
        handle.join().unwrap();
    }

    println!("Final count: {}",
counter.load(Ordering::SeqCst));
}
```

Atomic types are extremely fast and completely lock-free—but only suitable for simple data types. For anything more complex, always use a mutex.

Avoiding Deadlocks

A **deadlock** occurs when two or more threads are waiting on each other to release resources—and none of them can proceed. This typically happens when multiple mutexes are locked in an inconsistent order.

Let's look at a classic deadlock example:

```
use std::sync::{Arc, Mutex};
use std::thread;

fn main() {
    let lock_a = Arc::new(Mutex::new(()));
    let lock_b = Arc::new(Mutex::new(()));

    let a = Arc::clone(&lock_a);
    let b = Arc::clone(&lock_b);

    let t1 = thread::spawn(move || {
        let _a = a.lock().unwrap();
        // simulate work

std::thread::sleep(std::time::Duration::from_millis
(100));
        let _b = b.lock().unwrap();
```

66

```
        println!("Thread 1 acquired both locks");
    });

    let a = Arc::clone(&lock_a);
    let b = Arc::clone(&lock_b);

    let t2 = thread::spawn(move || {
        let _b = b.lock().unwrap();
        let _a = a.lock().unwrap(); // deadlock
risk here
        println!("Thread 2 acquired both locks");
    });

    t1.join().unwrap();
    t2.join().unwrap();
}
```

Here, thread 1 locks a and then tries to lock b, while thread 2 does the reverse. If both acquire their first lock before the second is available, they'll wait on each other forever.

Rust won't prevent this at compile time because it's a **logic issue**, not a safety issue. You're using synchronization properly—but in the wrong order.

To prevent this kind of deadlock:

Always acquire multiple locks in the **same order** across all threads.

Consider using a higher-level abstraction like a channel instead of shared locks.

Use tools like `try_lock()` if you want to implement timeout or fail-fast behavior.

Here's how to rewrite the above code to prevent deadlock by enforcing lock order:

```
use std::sync::{Arc, Mutex};
use std::thread;

fn main() {
    let lock_a = Arc::new(Mutex::new(()));
    let lock_b = Arc::new(Mutex::new(()));
```

```rust
    let a = Arc::clone(&lock_a);
    let b = Arc::clone(&lock_b);

    let t1 = thread::spawn(move || {
        let (_a, _b) = lock_in_order(&a, &b);
        println!("Thread 1 acquired both locks");
    });

    let a = Arc::clone(&lock_a);
    let b = Arc::clone(&lock_b);

    let t2 = thread::spawn(move || {
        let (_a, _b) = lock_in_order(&a, &b);
        println!("Thread 2 acquired both locks");
    });

    t1.join().unwrap();
    t2.join().unwrap();
}

fn lock_in_order<'a>(
    first: &'a Mutex<()>,
    second: &'a Mutex<()>,
) -> (std::sync::MutexGuard<'a, ()>,
std::sync::MutexGuard<'a, ()>) {
    let lock1 = first.lock().unwrap();
    let lock2 = second.lock().unwrap();
    (lock1, lock2)
}
```

By encapsulating the locking logic and always locking in the same order, you eliminate the chance of deadlock.

Exercise: Simulate and Prevent a Deadlock

Here's a deadlock-prone setup:

```rust
use std::sync::{Arc, Mutex};
use std::thread;

fn main() {
    let res1 = Arc::new(Mutex::new(()));
```

```rust
    let res2 = Arc::new(Mutex::new(()));

    let r1 = Arc::clone(&res1);
    let r2 = Arc::clone(&res2);

    let t1 = thread::spawn(move || {
        let _lock1 = r1.lock().unwrap();
        let _lock2 = r2.lock().unwrap();
        println!("Thread 1 finished");
    });

    let r1 = Arc::clone(&res1);
    let r2 = Arc::clone(&res2);

    let t2 = thread::spawn(move || {
        let _lock2 = r2.lock().unwrap();
        let _lock1 = r1.lock().unwrap();
        println!("Thread 2 finished");
    });

    t1.join().unwrap();
    t2.join().unwrap();
}
```

Task: Refactor this so both threads acquire the locks in the same order.

Concurrency is powerful, but it requires precision. Race conditions are dangerous because they silently corrupt your data. Deadlocks are dangerous because they freeze your program entirely. Rust helps you avoid both—either by preventing shared mutable access at compile time or by structuring your locking mechanisms clearly.

If you follow consistent locking patterns, use `Mutex` and atomics correctly, and avoid shared state when message passing would suffice, you can write concurrent Rust code that's fast, correct, and safe under pressure.

Chapter 5: System Interfaces and FFI

One of the key advantages of using Rust for systems programming is that you're not locked into just the abstractions provided by Rust itself. You can talk directly to the operating system. You can call native C APIs. You can link to existing libraries and use system calls just like you would in C or C++. That's because Rust was designed to be a **systems language** from the ground up.

This chapter is all about bridging Rust with the outside world—whether it's invoking raw system calls, using `libc`, working with the POSIX API, or linking to C libraries that have been around for decades. This is where we go beyond high-level safety and dig into the low-level hooks that make Rust truly viable for operating systems, device drivers, embedded firmware, and performance-critical native applications.

Making Direct System Calls

When you're working at the systems level, there are times when you need to go beyond the abstractions of a standard library. You need direct access to the operating system—to perform low-level tasks like working with file descriptors, sending signals, interacting with processes, or controlling device-level operations. These actions are handled through **system calls**, which are the gateway between user-space applications and the kernel.

Rust, being a systems language, fully supports making system calls. But it doesn't expose most of them directly in the standard library. Instead, Rust expects that you'll use an external interface like the `libc` crate, which provides bindings to standard C system calls, or `nix`, which offers Rust-friendly wrappers over those low-level calls.

A system call is a controlled transition from user space into the operating system's kernel. When your program needs to open a file, create a process, allocate memory, or send network data, it cannot do so directly—it must request the OS to perform the operation on its behalf.

In C, this typically happens through functions like `open()`, `read()`, `write()`, `fork()`, `execve()`, and so on. These functions are just user-space wrappers over the actual syscall mechanism.

In Rust, you can make the same calls using the `libc` crate, which exposes C's system functions as raw `extern` bindings.

Directly Writing to File Descriptors with `libc::write`

Let's start with something simple but fundamental: writing a message to standard output using the `write` system call.

```
use libc::{c_void, size_t, write};
use std::ffi::CString;

fn main() {
    let message = CString::new("Hello from a raw
system call!\n").unwrap();
    let ptr = message.as_ptr() as *const c_void;
    let len = message.to_bytes().len() as size_t;

    unsafe {
        write(1, ptr, len); // 1 is the file
descriptor for stdout
    }
}
```

Here's what's happening:

We use `CString` to create a null-terminated C-compatible string.

We extract a raw pointer (`as_ptr()`), cast it to `*const c_void`, and determine its length.

We call `write(fd, buffer, length)` where `fd = 1` (stdout).

This is done in an `unsafe` block, because system calls bypass Rust's memory guarantees.

Even this simple example teaches an important lesson: when you use raw system interfaces, you're responsible for ensuring pointer validity, memory alignment, and other correctness properties. Rust lets you opt in—but not silently.

Opening a File with `libc::open`, Reading with `libc::read`

Let's go a step further. Suppose you want to open a file and read data from it using raw system calls.

```rust
use libc::{c_void, close, open, read, O_RDONLY};
use std::ffi::CString;

fn main() {
    let filename =
CString::new("hello.txt").unwrap();

    let fd = unsafe { open(filename.as_ptr(),
O_RDONLY) };
    if fd < 0 {
        eprintln!("Failed to open file.");
        return;
    }

    let mut buffer = [0u8; 128];

    let bytes_read = unsafe {
        read(fd, buffer.as_mut_ptr() as *mut
c_void, buffer.len())
    };

    if bytes_read > 0 {
        let output =
String::from_utf8_lossy(&buffer[..bytes_read as
usize]);
        println!("File contents:\n{}", output);
    } else {
        eprintln!("Failed to read from file.");
    }

    unsafe {
        close(fd);
    }
}
```

Let's break this down:

We use `libc::open` with the `O_RDONLY` flag to open the file for reading.

We read into a stack-allocated byte buffer using `read`.

The buffer is then converted to a Rust `String` using `from_utf8_lossy`.

Finally, we call `close` to release the file descriptor.

This is a classic C-style interaction with the operating system—done in Rust, with more predictable behavior and better memory safety (even though it's wrapped in `unsafe`).

This approach is useful in bare-metal environments, custom operating systems, or embedded systems where the full standard library might not be available.

Working with errno and Error Handling

In C, most syscalls return a negative number to indicate an error and set a global variable called `errno`. In Rust, using `libc`, you access this via `*libc::__errno_location()` on Linux or `*libc::__error()` on macOS.

Let's try calling `open` on a non-existent file and check the error:

```
use libc::{c_char, errno, open, O_RDONLY};
use std::ffi::CString;

fn main() {
    let filename =
CString::new("does_not_exist.txt").unwrap();

    let fd = unsafe { open(filename.as_ptr() as
*const c_char, O_RDONLY) };
    if fd < 0 {
        let err_code = unsafe {
*libc::__errno_location() };
        println!("Failed to open file. errno: {}",
err_code);
    }
}
```

Always check the return values of system calls, and be prepared to handle errors. System programming is full of cases where things don't work the first time—permissions, unavailable resources, missing files, or race conditions during access.

Exercise: Manual System Call-Based Cat Utility

Write a small Rust program that:

Takes a filename as a command-line argument.

Opens it using `libc::open`.

Reads it using `libc::read`.

Prints it to stdout using `libc::write`.

Avoid using the Rust standard library for file handling—use only system calls.

Hint: You'll use:

`libc::open`

`libc::read`

`libc::write`

`libc::close`

`std::env::args()` to get the filename

Real-World Relevance

Why would you want to use raw system calls in Rust when higher-level crates exist?

You're building a minimal runtime (like in `no_std` environments).

You're writing an OS kernel, bootloader, or embedded firmware.

You need precise control over syscall parameters, memory layout, or performance.

You're interoperating with C codebases and need to match exact system behaviors.

You're porting or wrapping legacy C libraries with no high-level bindings available.

Using `libc` is the foundation. For ergonomics and cross-platform compatibility, you may choose to layer `nix` or `cap-std` on top later. But understanding how system calls work, and how to use them correctly in Rust, gives you ultimate flexibility and confidence when you're working close to the hardware or kernel.

When you make system calls in Rust, you're doing the real work—the kind that operating systems, drivers, servers, and low-level services depend on. You're working with raw file descriptors, byte buffers, and unfiltered OS feedback. That's why Rust requires you to mark this code `unsafe`. It doesn't mean the code is bad. It means *you* are now in charge of safety, and Rust will not make assumptions for you.

Working with C Libraries and External Code

One of the most important reasons Rust is practical for systems development is that it doesn't isolate you from existing native code. Instead, it lets you **interoperate** with it. That means you can use mature C libraries that already solve hard problems—like image processing, compression, encryption, or networking—without having to rewrite them in Rust. And you can do so with precise control, direct memory access, and full compatibility.

This is possible through Rust's **FFI**—Foreign Function Interface. FFI is the mechanism that allows Rust code to call functions written in C, and vice versa. If you're coming from a C or C++ background, this isn't foreign at all—you're just linking external binaries. But in Rust, you need to be a bit more explicit and careful, because safety and correctness still matter.

Calling a C Function from Rust

Let's start with a small C library. Save this in a file called `mathlib.c`:

```c
// mathlib.c
int add(int a, int b) {
    return a + b;
}
```

Compile it using `gcc`:

```
gcc -c mathlib.c -o mathlib.o
```

```
ar rcs libmathlib.a mathlib.o
```

This produces a static library file: `libmathlib.a`. Rust can link to this.

Now, write a Rust file to call this function:

```rust
// main.rs
extern "C" {
    fn add(a: i32, b: i32) -> i32;
}

fn main() {
    unsafe {
        let result = add(5, 7);
        println!("The sum is: {}", result);
    }
}
```

Next, you need to configure your project to link with the library. Create a `build.rs` file in your crate root:

```rust
// build.rs
fn main() {
    println!("cargo:rustc-link-search=.");
    println!("cargo:rustc-link-lib=static=mathlib");
}
```

And update `Cargo.toml` to use the build script:

```
[package]
```

```
name = "ffi_example"
```

```
version = "0.1.0"
```

```
edition = "2021"
```

```
build = "build.rs"
```

Now when you run `cargo run`, it compiles and links correctly.

Note: `extern "C"` tells Rust to use the C calling convention. Without it, the function's symbol name might not match, and the call could fail or produce unpredictable behavior.

Passing Strings and Pointers

Calling C functions that accept strings is a bit more involved. C strings are null-terminated (\0) and stored as raw pointers. Rust strings (`String` or `&str`) are not null-terminated and are stored with a length, so you have to explicitly convert them.

Let's say you have a C function like this:

```
// greet.c
#include <stdio.h>

void greet(const char* name) {
    printf("Hello, %s!\n", name);
}
```

Compile it into a static lib:

```
gcc -c greet.c -o greet.o
```

```
ar rcs libgreet.a greet.o
```

In Rust, you'd write:

```
use std::ffi::CString;

extern "C" {
    fn greet(name: *const i8);
}

fn main() {
    let name = CString::new("Rustacean").unwrap();
    unsafe {
        greet(name.as_ptr());
    }
}
```

Key points:

`CString::new()` ensures the Rust string is null-terminated.

`as_ptr()` gets the raw pointer, which is passed to the C function.

You must use `unsafe` because Rust can't guarantee what happens once control leaves safe memory management.

This pattern is standard any time you're sending text or buffers into C code.

Returning Strings from C (and Handling Ownership)

Let's suppose the C side allocates and returns a string:

```c
// hello.c
#include <stdlib.h>
#include <string.h>

char* hello() {
    char* msg = malloc(64);
    strcpy(msg, "Greetings from C!");
    return msg;
}

void release(char* ptr) {
    free(ptr);
}
```

And in Rust:

```rust
use std::ffi::CStr;

extern "C" {
    fn hello() -> *mut i8;
    fn release(ptr: *mut i8);
}

fn main() {
    unsafe {
        let raw = hello();
        let c_str = CStr::from_ptr(raw);
        let message = c_str.to_str().unwrap();
        println!("Received: {}", message);
        release(raw);
    }
```

```
}
```

Here, we:

Receive a pointer from `hello()`.

Convert it using `CStr::from_ptr` and `.to_str()`.

Print the message.

Call `release()` to free the memory. This is crucial—you must always match allocators. If C allocated it, C must free it.

Making Rust Functions Callable from C

You might also want to go the other way—expose Rust functions to be called from C. This is useful if you're migrating a legacy C codebase incrementally or building Rust-based libraries for C consumers.

Here's a Rust function exposed to C:

```
#[no_mangle]

pub extern "C" fn multiply(a: i32, b: i32) -> i32 {

    a * b

}
```

Compile your crate into a staticlib:

```
In Cargo.toml:

[lib]

name = "mylib"

crate-type = ["staticlib"]
```

Then from C:

```
// caller.c
#include <stdio.h>
```

```
extern int multiply(int, int);

int main() {
    printf("Result: %d\n", multiply(3, 4));
    return 0;
}
```

Link the generated `libmylib.a` with `gcc`:

`gcc caller.c -Ltarget/release -lmylib -o caller`

Your C application now uses a function compiled from Rust.

Exercise: Wrapping a C Library

Build a minimal C library:

```
// double.c

int double_value(int x) {

    return 2 * x;

}
```

Compile it to `libdouble.a`. Then:

Write a Rust wrapper function in a safe module.

Create a `build.rs` to link the static library.

Use the wrapper in your `main()` and print the result.

Safety Considerations

Whenever you're working across the FFI boundary:

Always validate input and output values.

Be very careful with pointers—null, dangling, or misaligned pointers are undefined behavior.

Never assume the size or layout of a struct is identical on both sides unless you control both definitions.

Use `#[repr(C)]` on Rust structs if you're sharing them with C.

Example:

```
#[repr(C)]
pub struct Point {
    pub x: i32,
    pub y: i32,
}
```

This guarantees that `Point` has a C-compatible layout.

Rust doesn't hide you from native code—it encourages you to interface with it cleanly and explicitly. Whether you're leveraging decades of C libraries, integrating with system APIs, or building a bridge to a legacy system, Rust's FFI gives you complete control without giving up safety where it matters.

By learning how to call C functions, pass pointers and strings, and expose Rust APIs to external programs, you gain the ability to build software that fits into any low-level environment—on embedded systems, on servers, or in operating systems.

Using the `libc` and `nix` Crates

When you're writing systems-level code in Rust, the line between Rust and C is not just something you can cross—it's something you often *need* to cross. Operating systems, device drivers, and low-level APIs have all been historically written in C, and interacting with them requires bindings that speak their language. The standard Rust library only goes so far; it stops short of exposing raw system calls or POSIX interfaces directly. That's where the `libc` and `nix` crates come in.

These crates allow your Rust code to talk directly to the underlying system in a way that's safe, predictable, and as idiomatic as possible—depending on how much abstraction you want. `libc` gives you thin bindings to C functions. `nix` builds on `libc` and gives you structured, type-safe, and error-checked Rust wrappers.

We're going to break down how both work, how to use them properly, and

What the `libc` Crate Offers

The `libc` crate is the foundational FFI layer between Rust and C. It provides **raw, low-level access** to C system calls and types. You can call `open`, `read`, `write`, `mmap`, `fork`, `exec`, and many other functions—just like in C. You get direct access to types like `pid_t`, `size_t`, `mode_t`, `c_void`, and more.

Here's a simple example that uses `libc` to write directly to `stdout` using the `write` system call:

```rust
use libc::{c_void, size_t, write};
use std::ffi::CString;

fn main() {
    let message = CString::new("Hello from
libc!\n").unwrap();
    let ptr = message.as_ptr() as *const c_void;
    let len = message.to_bytes().len() as size_t;

    unsafe {
        write(1, ptr, len);
    }
}
```

This is exactly what you'd do in C using `write(1, message, len)`, except wrapped in Rust's stricter type system. Note that the call must be in an `unsafe` block because Rust can't verify what happens once the system call executes.

You can also use `libc` to access file operations:

```rust
use libc::{open, read, close, O_RDONLY};
use std::ffi::CString;

fn main() {
    let filename =
CString::new("hello.txt").unwrap();

    let fd = unsafe { open(filename.as_ptr(),
O_RDONLY) };
    if fd < 0 {
        eprintln!("Failed to open file");
        return;
    }
```

```rust
    let mut buffer = [0u8; 128];
    let n = unsafe { read(fd, buffer.as_mut_ptr()
as *mut _, buffer.len()) };

    if n > 0 {
        println!("{}",
String::from_utf8_lossy(&buffer[..n as usize]));
    }

    unsafe {
        close(fd);
    }
}
```

With `libc`, you're writing code just like in C. It's fast and direct—but also dangerous if you're not careful. There's no error handling abstraction, and you have to remember to check return values and match types yourself.

What the `nix` Crate Adds

The `nix` crate builds on `libc` by wrapping these raw system calls into safe, idiomatic Rust. It takes care of the boilerplate, like converting error codes to `Result<T, nix::Error>`, handling types properly, and abstracting unsafe calls into safe ones.

Here's the same example rewritten using `nix`:

```rust
use nix::unistd::{read, write, close};
use nix::fcntl::open;
use nix::sys::stat::Mode;
use nix::fcntl::OFlag;
use std::os::unix::io::RawFd;

fn main() {
    let fd: RawFd = match open("hello.txt",
OFlag::O_RDONLY, Mode::empty()) {
        Ok(file) => file,
        Err(e) => {
            eprintln!("Failed to open file: {}",
e);
            return;
        }
```

```rust
    };

    let mut buffer = [0u8; 128];

    match read(fd, &mut buffer) {
        Ok(n) => {
            let s =
String::from_utf8_lossy(&buffer[..n]);
            println!("Read: {}", s);
        }
        Err(e) => eprintln!("Failed to read: {}",
e),
    }

    if let Err(e) = close(fd) {
        eprintln!("Failed to close file: {}", e);
    }
}
```

This version is:

Safer: it doesn't require `unsafe`.

Clearer: all error handling is explicit and structured.

Portable: `nix` works across Linux, macOS, and BSD systems, abstracting platform-specific behavior.

In short, `nix` makes system programming in Rust feel like idiomatic Rust, not like C with extra type annotations.

Example: Forking and Executing a Child Process

Using `libc`:

```rust
use libc::{fork, execlp, _exit};

fn main() {
    unsafe {
        let pid = fork();
        if pid == 0 {
            execlp("ls\0".as_ptr() as *const _,
"ls\0".as_ptr() as *const _,
std::ptr::null::<*const i8>());
```

```
                _exit(1);
        } else if pid > 0 {
                println!("Spawned child with PID {}",
pid);
        } else {
                eprintln!("Fork failed");
        }
    }
}
```

Using `nix`:

```
use nix::unistd::{fork, ForkResult, execvp};
use std::ffi::CString;

fn main() {
    match unsafe { fork() } {
        Ok(ForkResult::Child) => {
            let cmd = CString::new("ls").unwrap();
            let args = [cmd.clone()];
            execvp(&cmd, &args).expect("exec
failed");
        }
        Ok(ForkResult::Parent { child }) => {
            println!("Spawned child with PID: {}",
child);
        }
        Err(err) => {
            eprintln!("Fork failed: {}", err);
        }
    }
}
```

The `nix` version is cleaner, easier to read, and safer. It uses `CString` to manage null-terminated arguments and automatically returns a proper `Result`.

Real-World Use: Memory Mapping

Memory-mapped files are often used in high-performance systems programming. You can use `libc::mmap`, but it's messy. Here's how it looks with `nix`:

```
use nix::sys::mman::{mmap, MapFlags, ProtFlags};
```

```rust
use std::fs::File;
use std::os::unix::io::AsRawFd;
use std::ptr;

fn main() {
    let file = File::open("hello.txt").unwrap();
    let len = file.metadata().unwrap().len() as
usize;

    let data = unsafe {
        mmap(
            ptr::null_mut(),
            len,
            ProtFlags::PROT_READ,
            MapFlags::MAP_PRIVATE,
            file.as_raw_fd(),
            0,
        )
    }.unwrap();

    let content = unsafe {
        std::slice::from_raw_parts(data as *const
u8, len)
    };

    println!("{}",
String::from_utf8_lossy(content));
}
```

This code maps a file into memory, reads from it using a slice, and prints the contents—without copying it into a buffer manually. `nix` makes the call feel just like using Rust standard APIs.

Exercise: File Descriptor Echo Server (with nix)

Write a minimal TCP echo server that:

Listens on a port.

Accepts a connection.

Reads from the socket and writes back the same data.

Use:

`nix::sys::socket`

`nix::unistd::read` and `write`

`nix::fcntl` for setting socket options if needed

This exercise demonstrates how `nix` enables network programming without needing external libraries like `tokio` or `mio`.

When to Use `libc` vs `nix`

Use `libc` when:

You need direct control over system calls.

You're working on extremely low-level or embedded code.

You need compatibility with `no_std`.

Use `nix` when:

You want safe, idiomatic Rust with error handling.

You need high-level access to Unix features like signals, sockets, pipes, or memory-mapping.

You value readability and safety over raw flexibility.

Both have their place. In fact, `nix` itself is built on top of `libc`.

`libc` gives you the power to talk to the system like C does. `nix` gives you the tools to do it in a way that feels like Rust—safe, composable, and readable. Understanding both gives you total control over system behavior, whether you're tweaking a syscall interface, building a POSIX-compliant shell, or writing performance-critical infrastructure software.

By using `libc` and `nix` effectively, you can write systems code that is both fast and correct, that interops cleanly with existing C libraries, and that leverages decades of low-level software infrastructure while staying within Rust's safe design principles.

Chapter 6: Filesystems and Process Control

When you're building systems software, you're not writing isolated logic—you're interacting with the operating system itself. Whether it's reading and writing to files, inspecting system information, spawning subprocesses, or responding to signals, you need a strong grip on how to work with the OS as an active participant, not just a user.

This chapter is focused on precisely that—how to work with the **filesystem**, how to interact with **system resources** like memory and file descriptors, and how to safely control **processes, signals, and permissions** using Rust. You'll learn how to read and write structured binary data, how to pull useful system state, and how to manage other programs from within your own.

Rust doesn't hide these low-level interactions from you. Instead, it gives you the tools to do them safely and clearly—through the standard library, through system crates like `nix`, and when needed, through raw system calls.

Reading and Writing Binary Data

When you're building systems software, you're almost guaranteed to work with raw bytes at some point. This might be reading structured data from a device, writing logs to a custom format, interacting with a file format that isn't plain text, or managing in-memory serialization between processes. These aren't strings or JSON—they're structured binary formats with specific byte layouts, endianness, and strict expectations. And in Rust, you can handle all of that safely and efficiently without giving up control.

This section is about building a strong and practical understanding of how to read and write binary data in Rust. We'll look at how data is represented in memory, how to convert between native types and byte buffers, and how to write and read from files without losing any precision or structure. You'll see real examples of how to deal with primitive values, fixed-size structs, and raw byte manipulation in a way that's both idiomatic and correct.

Writing Raw Binary Data to a File

Rust's standard library makes it easy to write raw bytes to disk. If you have a primitive type like a `u32`, you can serialize it into a byte array using `.to_le_bytes()` or `.to_be_bytes()`, depending on whether you want little-endian or big-endian representation.

Here's how you might write several integers into a binary file:

```
use std::fs::File;
use std::io::{Write, Result};

fn main() -> Result<()> {
    let mut file = File::create("numbers.bin")?;

    let values: [u32; 4] = [100, 200, 300, 400];

    for val in &values {
        let bytes = val.to_le_bytes(); // convert
to little-endian
        file.write_all(&bytes)?;        // write the
raw bytes
    }

    Ok(())
}
```

Each call to `to_le_bytes()` converts the integer into an array of 4 bytes. When you write those bytes to the file, they go exactly as-is, without any formatting or delimiters. This is how most system-level formats store structured data—compact and exact.

You can use this technique with other fixed-size types too: `i32`, `f32`, `u64`, etc.

Reading Binary Data from a File

Reading binary data back is just the reverse process: read the raw bytes into a buffer, and reconstruct your type from that buffer using functions like `from_le_bytes()`.

Here's how you can read the `u32` values we wrote earlier:

```
use std::fs::File;
use std::io::{Read, Result};
```

```
fn main() -> Result<()> {
    let mut file = File::open("numbers.bin")?;
    let mut buffer = [0u8; 4]; // u32 is 4 bytes

    while file.read_exact(&mut buffer).is_ok() {
        let num = u32::from_le_bytes(buffer);
        println!("Read: {}", num);
    }

    Ok(())
}
```

read_exact() ensures we always read the full 4 bytes needed for a u32. If we reach the end of the file, the read will fail and the loop will stop gracefully. This gives you a clean way to scan through a binary file, one structured item at a time.

Reading and Writing Structs as Binary

Now let's say you're working with a binary file format that stores fixed-size records—each with fields like a timestamp, a value, and a flag. You might want to define a Rust struct and read/write instances of that struct in raw form.

Rust doesn't let you do that directly (for good reason—memory layout isn't guaranteed to match across platforms), but you can define your own layout using #[repr(C)] and convert manually.

Here's how:

```
#[repr(C)]

#[derive(Debug, Copy, Clone)]

struct Record {

    timestamp: u64,

    value: f32,

    flag: u8,

}
```

To write this to a file:

```
use std::fs::File;
use std::io::Write;
use std::mem;

fn main() -> std::io::Result<()> {
    let mut file = File::create("record.bin")?;

    let record = Record {
        timestamp: 1695840000,
        value: 42.5,
        flag: 1,
    };

    let ptr = &record as *const Record as *const
u8;
    let size = mem::size_of::<Record>();

    let bytes = unsafe {
std::slice::from_raw_parts(ptr, size) };

    file.write_all(bytes)?;
    Ok(())
}
```

Important: this technique is only safe if:

The struct has #[repr(C)]

It contains only simple types

You're aware of padding between fields

Reading it back:

```
use std::fs::File;
use std::io::Read;
use std::mem;

fn main() -> std::io::Result<()> {
    let mut file = File::open("record.bin")?;
    let mut buffer = vec![0u8;
mem::size_of::<Record>()];

    file.read_exact(&mut buffer)?;
```

```
    let ptr = buffer.as_ptr() as *const Record;

    let record = unsafe { *ptr };

    println!("{:?}", record);

    Ok(())
}
```

This approach is fast and works well when you control both ends of the file format. If you're working with a standard format or variable-length records, you'll want to use serialization formats or hand-parse fields manually.

Dealing with Endianness

If you're working on a system where byte order matters—such as when writing network protocols, embedded logs, or binary formats defined by external systems—you need to pay attention to **endianness**.

Rust provides `.to_le_bytes()` and `.to_be_bytes()` for all primitive integer and floating-point types:

```
let n: u16 = 0x1234;

let be = n.to_be_bytes(); // [0x12, 0x34]

let le = n.to_le_bytes(); // [0x34, 0x12]
```

And the reverse:

```
let from_be = u16::from_be_bytes(be);

let from_le = u16::from_le_bytes(le);
```

This makes it easy to work with systems that define specific byte ordering (like most networking protocols, which use big-endian).

Exercise: Create a Simple Binary Log Format

Define a record like this:

```
#[repr(C)]
struct LogEntry {
    timestamp: u64,
```

```
    level: u8,
    message_len: u8,
}
```

Write a binary log file where each entry starts with a fixed-size header (`LogEntry`) followed by a variable-length UTF-8 message string.

Your task:

Create and write multiple entries to a file.

Read them back one at a time, parsing the struct and reading the correct number of bytes for each message.

Print each entry as: `timestamp [level]: message`

This mirrors the structure of many real-world formats, like journal logs or compact event recorders.

Binary data isn't abstract—it's the raw, byte-for-byte structure that the system reads and writes directly. When you control those bytes, you control the interface. Rust gives you full access to that level of programming—but it asks you to be careful. And that's the right trade.

You'll always know when you're casting pointers or reading buffers. The compiler won't silently reinterpret data. But when you need to lay out bytes with precision, read values exactly as they were written, or build formats that match external specs, Rust has your back.

With this foundation, you can confidently write file parsers, memory mappers, network protocol encoders, and storage engines—knowing that what you see is what you wrote.

Accessing System Resources

When you're building systems software, you're not working in isolation from the machine. You're right in the thick of it—reading from the filesystem, accessing environment variables, monitoring CPU and memory usage, inspecting file descriptors, and interacting with operating system features like process IDs and capabilities. These are not optional details—they are core parts of system behavior.

Rust gives you powerful tools to query and control these system resources directly. You can do it through the standard library where possible, or fall back on crates like `libc`, `nix`, or platform-specific modules like `/proc` (on Linux) to get full access.

In this section, you'll learn how to:

Access environment variables and process metadata

List and inspect file descriptors

Query memory and CPU usage

Check system uptime, hostname, and other runtime-level details

Working with Environment Variables

Environment variables are a primary way to configure software without hardcoding values. They're used to define paths, ports, API keys, and even behavior flags. Rust makes working with them straightforward using the `std::env` module.

To read a specific environment variable:

```rust
use std::env;

fn main() {
    match env::var("HOME") {
        Ok(home) => println!("User home directory:
{}", home),
        Err(err) => eprintln!("Could not read HOME:
{}", err),
    }
}
```

This returns a `Result<String, VarError>`, so you can handle missing or invalid variables safely.

To set or override an environment variable:

```rust
use std::env;

fn main() {
    env::set_var("RUST_LOG_LEVEL", "debug");
```

94

```
    let level =
env::var("RUST_LOG_LEVEL").unwrap();
    println!("Logging level is now: {}", level);
}
```

Listing all environment variables can be useful when debugging or building dynamic configurations:

```
use std::env;

fn main() {
    for (key, value) in env::vars() {
        println!("{} = {}", key, value);
    }
}
```

This gives you full visibility into what your process was launched with.

Getting Process and User Metadata

You often need to know what process you're running as—particularly if you're dealing with permissions, signal handling, or containerized environments.

Current process ID:

```
fn main() {

    let pid = std::process::id();

    println!("This process ID is: {}", pid);

}
```

If you want more detailed info—like real and effective UID/GID, use the `nix` crate:

```
use nix::unistd::{getuid, geteuid, getgid,
getegid};


fn main() {
```

95

```
    println!("Real UID: {}", getuid());

    println!("Effective UID: {}", geteuid());

    println!("Real GID: {}", getgid());

    println!("Effective GID: {}", getegid());

}
```

This is critical when you're dropping privileges, running in a sandbox, or checking whether your process has sufficient rights to access protected files or devices.

Inspecting File Descriptors (Linux)

In Linux, every open file, socket, pipe, or device in your process is associated with a file descriptor (FD). These are visible via /proc/self/fd, and they're incredibly useful for debugging resource leaks, monitoring socket usage, or building advanced utilities like debuggers or sandboxes.

Here's how to list all open file descriptors for your current process:

```
use std::fs;

fn main() {
    let entries =
fs::read_dir("/proc/self/fd").unwrap();

    for entry in entries {
        let entry = entry.unwrap();
        let path = entry.path();
        let target =
fs::read_link(&path).unwrap_or_else(|_|
"unreadable".into());

        println!("{} -> {}", path.display(),
target.display());
    }
}
```

Each entry in `/proc/self/fd/` is a symlink pointing to the actual file, socket, or pipe. You can see exactly which files are open, what sockets are in use, and which pipes are still active.

This kind of introspection is invaluable when troubleshooting systems programs under load.

Accessing Memory and CPU Information

Want to see how much memory your system has, or how much your process is consuming? You can parse `/proc/meminfo` and `/proc/self/status`.

Here's a simple way to print the memory stats:

```
use std::fs;

fn main() {
    let contents =
fs::read_to_string("/proc/meminfo").unwrap();
    for line in contents.lines().take(5) {
        println!("{}", line);
    }
}
```

And for process-specific memory:

```
fn main() {
    let status =
std::fs::read_to_string("/proc/self/status").unwrap
();

    for line in status.lines() {
        if line.starts_with("VmRSS") ||
line.starts_with("VmSize") {
            println!("{}", line);
        }
    }
}
```

You can also get CPU stats from `/proc/stat` or use crates like `sysinfo` for a cross-platform solution with richer abstraction:

```
# Cargo.toml
```

```
[dependencies]
sysinfo = "0.30"
use sysinfo::{System, SystemExt};

fn main() {
    let mut sys = System::new_all();
    sys.refresh_all();

    println!("Total memory: {} KB",
sys.total_memory());
    println!("Used memory: {} KB",
sys.used_memory());
    println!("Available CPUs: {}",
sys.cpus().len());
}
```

This works on Linux, macOS, and Windows, and is ideal when building monitoring tools.

Checking Uptime, Hostname, and Load

Need to get the system uptime?

```
fn main() {
    let uptime =
std::fs::read_to_string("/proc/uptime").unwrap();
    let seconds: f64 =
uptime.split_whitespace().next().unwrap().parse().u
nwrap();
    println!("System uptime: {:.2} seconds",
seconds);
}
```

Want the hostname?

```
use std::fs;

fn main() {
    let hostname =
fs::read_to_string("/proc/sys/kernel/hostname").unw
rap();
    println!("Hostname: {}", hostname.trim());
}
```

For system load average (1, 5, and 15 minutes):

```
fn main() {

    let load =
std::fs::read_to_string("/proc/loadavg").unwrap();

    println!("Load average: {}", load);

}
```

These values are handy for building status dashboards, logging, or autoscaling logic.

Exercise: Build a Process Inspector

Write a small tool that:

Prints the current process PID

Shows real and effective UID/GID

Lists open file descriptors

Prints memory usage (VmRSS and VmSize)

Displays system uptime and load average

Bonus: Accept a `--json` flag and output everything in JSON using `serde_json`.

This exercise combines everything from this section and prepares you for building tools like system agents, debuggers, or diagnostic utilities.

When you're writing software that doesn't just *run on* a system, but actually *interacts with* the system, you need to be able to see and control what's happening at the process and environment level. That includes inspecting memory, checking open files, reading environment variables, understanding who your process is running as, and tracking system-wide conditions like load and uptime.

Rust gives you clean and safe access to all of these without sacrificing control. You can use the standard library for high-level tasks, parse `/proc` for raw insights, or drop into `nix` and `libc` when you need precision.

With these tools, you're not writing isolated code—you're writing software that responds to the system, observes it, and behaves accordingly.

Managing Processes, Signals, and Permissions

Controlling processes is a fundamental part of systems programming. Whether you're spawning worker processes, managing subprocess lifecycles, catching system signals like SIGTERM or SIGINT, or modifying the permissions of your own program for security, you need direct, reliable access to process and OS-level behavior.

Rust gives you structured, type-safe tools to do all of this without falling into the traps that make it dangerous in other languages. You can launch new commands, interact with their standard streams, monitor them, and even trap asynchronous signals cleanly—all with compile-time guarantees where possible, and clearly marked unsafe only where necessary.

Spawning and Managing Subprocesses

Rust's standard library gives you the **std::process::**Command API for spawning new processes. It's designed to be safe and ergonomic, and it covers most common use cases.

Here's how to run a simple command:

```
use std::process::Command;

fn main() {
    let status = Command::new("echo")
        .arg("Hello from subprocess")
        .status()
        .expect("Failed to execute process");

    println!("Subprocess exited with status: {}",
status);
}
```

You can also capture the output:

```
use std::process::Command;
```

```rust
fn main() {
    let output = Command::new("ls")
        .arg("-1")
        .output()
        .expect("Failed to run command");

    println!("stdout:\n{}",
String::from_utf8_lossy(&output.stdout));
    println!("stderr:\n{}",
String::from_utf8_lossy(&output.stderr));
    println!("exit code: {}",
output.status.code().unwrap_or(-1));
}
```

The `Command` builder allows you to configure:

Arguments

Environment variables

Working directory

Input/output redirection

Whether to wait or run asynchronously

Launching a command and redirecting its input and output:

```rust
use std::process::{Command, Stdio};

fn main() {
    let mut child = Command::new("grep")
        .arg("rust")
        .stdin(Stdio::piped())
        .stdout(Stdio::piped())
        .spawn()
        .expect("Failed to start grep");

    {
        let stdin =
child.stdin.as_mut().expect("Failed to open
stdin");
        use std::io::Write;
```

```
        writeln!(stdin,
"rust\njava\nc++").unwrap();
    }

    let output =
child.wait_with_output().expect("Failed to read
output");

    println!("Matching lines:\n{}",
String::from_utf8_lossy(&output.stdout));
}
```

This gives you powerful process control, suitable for scripting, pipeline construction, or task launching.

Forking and Executing (UNIX)

For low-level process control—like implementing your own init, service launcher, or shell—you'll want to use nix.

```
use nix::unistd::{fork, execvp, ForkResult};
use std::ffi::CString;

fn main() {
    match unsafe { fork() } {
        Ok(ForkResult::Child) => {
            let cmd = CString::new("ls").unwrap();
            let args = [cmd.clone()];
            execvp(&cmd, &args).expect("exec
failed");
        }
        Ok(ForkResult::Parent { child }) => {
            println!("Spawned child with PID: {}",
child);
        }
        Err(err) => {
            eprintln!("Fork failed: {}", err);
        }
    }
}
```

Here:

`fork()` creates a new process.

`execvp()` replaces the child's memory with a new program.

`ForkResult` tells you whether you're in the parent or child.

This is exactly how shells and process supervisors work.

Catching and Responding to Signals

In systems programming, you often need to handle asynchronous signals—like `SIGINT` (Ctrl+C), `SIGTERM` (termination), or `SIGHUP` (hangup). Rust doesn't have built-in signal handling in `std`, but you can use the `signal-hook` crate to do it cleanly and safely.

First, add it to `Cargo.toml`:

[dependencies]

signal-hook = "0.3"

Then:

```
use signal_hook::consts::SIGINT;
use signal_hook::iterator::Signals;

fn main() {
    let mut signals =
Signals::new(&[SIGINT]).expect("Failed to set up
signal handler");

    println!("Waiting for SIGINT (Ctrl+C)...");

    for signal in signals.forever() {
        println!("Received signal: {}", signal);
        break;
    }

    println!("Exiting gracefully");
}
```

This creates a blocking iterator that waits for registered signals and handles them synchronously. This is ideal for graceful shutdown, cleanup, or interrupt handling.

Sending Signals to Other Processes

You can also send signals using `nix::sys::signal`:

```rust
use nix::sys::signal::{kill, Signal};
use nix::unistd::Pid;

fn main() {
    let target_pid = Pid::from_raw(12345); //
Replace with an actual PID
    match kill(target_pid, Signal::SIGTERM) {
        Ok(_) => println!("Signal sent"),
        Err(err) => eprintln!("Failed to send
signal: {}", err),
    }
}
```

This is commonly used in supervisors or daemons that need to manage other processes.

Adjusting Permissions (UIDs and GIDs)

Sometimes your process needs to drop privileges after initialization—for example, when a daemon starts as root but should run as a limited user for security.

Use `nix::unistd::setuid()` and `setgid()`:

```rust
use nix::unistd::{setuid, setgid, Uid, Gid};

fn main() {
    let uid = Uid::from_raw(1000);
    let gid = Gid::from_raw(1000);

    if let Err(err) = setgid(gid) {
        eprintln!("Failed to set GID: {}", err);
        return;
    }

    if let Err(err) = setuid(uid) {
        eprintln!("Failed to set UID: {}", err);
        return;
    }
```

```
    println!("Running as UID {}, GID {}", uid,
gid);
}
```

This is essential when running system services that must protect themselves from privilege escalation.

Exercise: Graceful Worker Process

Write a Rust program that:

Spawns a long-running subprocess (`sleep 100`)

Listens for `SIGINT`

Sends a `SIGTERM` to the subprocess when the signal arrives

Waits for the subprocess to exit

Prints a clean shutdown message

This is exactly how process supervisors and graceful service shutdowns are implemented.

If your program interacts with other programs, runs system commands, supervises child processes, or needs to respond to operating system signals, you need tools that give you fine-grained control over process creation, signal routing, and permission handling. Rust gives you just that—with a combination of safe high-level APIs and system-level crates like `nix` and `signal-hook`.

You're not relying on wrappers. You're interacting with the OS directly—with clarity, safety, and full control over what your program does and how it behaves.

Chapter 7: Building Networked Applications

Systems software today rarely runs in isolation. Whether it's a daemon listening for commands, a client fetching updates from a remote service, or a microservice talking to others in a distributed system, network communication is fundamental. Writing software that listens for TCP connections, sends UDP packets, handles hundreds of concurrent clients, and speaks secure, structured protocols is what brings your code to life—over the wire.

Rust gives you robust, reliable tools for building networked applications—both at the low-level socket interface and at the higher layers of abstraction with asynchronous runtimes like **Tokio**. In this chapter, we'll walk through everything you need to write real network software: raw socket programming, building concurrent servers, and writing secure protocols with proper error handling.

TCP/UDP Socket Programming

Socket programming is one of the most foundational skills in systems development. It allows programs to communicate across networks—locally or over the internet—by sending and receiving bytes through well-defined protocols. The most commonly used protocols in this space are **TCP** and **UDP**. TCP offers reliable, ordered, and error-checked delivery of a stream of bytes, while UDP is faster but does not guarantee delivery, order, or integrity.

Rust provides strong support for low-level socket programming through the `std::net` module. This standard interface allows you to work directly with TCP and UDP sockets, giving you full control over how data is transmitted and received. Unlike many high-level abstractions in other languages, Rust keeps things explicit and safe, helping you avoid common bugs while still maintaining close control of the system.

Writing a Basic TCP Client

A TCP client connects to a server, sends some data, and waits for a response. In Rust, this is done using the `TcpStream` type. Here's a simple, functional client:

```rust
use std::net::TcpStream;
use std::io::{Write, Read};

fn main() {
    let mut stream =
TcpStream::connect("127.0.0.1:8000")
        .expect("Failed to connect to server");

    stream.write_all(b"Hello from
client").expect("Failed to send data");

    let mut buffer = [0u8; 128];
    let size = stream.read(&mut
buffer).expect("Failed to read data");

    println!("Received: {}",
String::from_utf8_lossy(&buffer[..size]));
}
```

This program establishes a connection with the server at `127.0.0.1:8000`, sends a message, waits for a response, and prints whatever it receives. All operations use blocking I/O.

Writing a TCP Server That Handles One Client at a Time

Now let's look at a basic server using `TcpListener`. It binds to an address and waits for clients to connect:

```rust
use std::net::TcpListener;
use std::io::{Read, Write};

fn main() {
    let listener =
TcpListener::bind("127.0.0.1:8000")
        .expect("Failed to bind to port");

    println!("Server running on 127.0.0.1:8000");

    for stream in listener.incoming() {
        match stream {
            Ok(mut stream) => {
                println!("Client connected: {}",
stream.peer_addr().unwrap());
```

```
                let mut buffer = [0u8; 128];
                let size = stream.read(&mut
buffer).unwrap();

                println!("Received: {}",
String::from_utf8_lossy(&buffer[..size]));

                stream.write_all(b"Hello from
server").unwrap();
            }
            Err(e) => {
                eprintln!("Connection failed: {}",
e);
            }
        }
    }
}
```

This handles one client per loop iteration. It reads the incoming data, prints it, and sends a response. Once that client disconnects, it waits for the next.
This setup works well for simple applications but is not scalable for multiple simultaneous clients. For that, you'd use threads or async I/O (covered in a later section).

Sending and Receiving with UDP

UDP sockets are connectionless. You don't establish a connection—you send a message to a specific address and port, and the recipient reads it from the socket.

Here's a UDP sender:

```
use std::net::UdpSocket;

fn main() {
    let socket =
UdpSocket::bind("0.0.0.0:0").expect("Failed to bind
to socket");

    socket.send_to(b"ping",
"127.0.0.1:9000").expect("Failed to send");
```

```
    }
```

This socket is bound to an ephemeral port (assigned automatically by the OS), and it sends a message to `127.0.0.1:9000`.

On the receiving end, a UDP server might look like this:

```
use std::net::UdpSocket;

fn main() {
    let socket =
UdpSocket::bind("127.0.0.1:9000").expect("Could not
bind UDP socket");

    let mut buffer = [0u8; 128];

    println!("UDP server listening on
127.0.0.1:9000");

    loop {
        let (size, sender) = socket.recv_from(&mut
buffer).expect("Failed to receive");
        println!("Received {} bytes from {}: {}",
size, sender,
String::from_utf8_lossy(&buffer[..size]));

        socket.send_to(b"PONG",
sender).expect("Failed to send response");
    }
}
```

This continuously receives data and responds to the sender with a "PONG". Because UDP does not maintain a connection, every message must include both the data and the address it's sent to or received from.

Handling Errors and Blocking Behavior

All the operations shown so far are **blocking**. That means the call to `read`, `write`, `recv`, or `send` will block the thread until the operation completes. For interactive or responsive programs, you must either use non-blocking I/O, spawn threads, or transition to an async model.

Let's say you want to set a timeout on socket operations:

109

```
use std::net::TcpStream;
use std::time::Duration;

fn main() {
    let mut stream =
TcpStream::connect("127.0.0.1:8000")
        .expect("Could not connect");


stream.set_read_timeout(Some(Duration::from_secs(5)
))
        .expect("Failed to set timeout");

    let mut buffer = [0u8; 128];
    match stream.read(&mut buffer) {
        Ok(size) => println!("Received: {}",
String::from_utf8_lossy(&buffer[..size])),
        Err(e) => eprintln!("Timed out or failed:
{}", e),
    }
}
```

This is essential for preventing your application from hanging forever if the other side is unresponsive.

Exercise: Build a UDP Echo Pair

Write two programs:

A **UDP server** that binds to `127.0.0.1:7000`, reads incoming messages, prints them, and sends them back to the sender.

A **UDP client** that sends a user-defined message to `127.0.0.1:7000`, waits for a response, and prints the reply.

Test them by running the server in one terminal and the client in another.

To take this further:

Make the server drop half of the messages randomly to simulate packet loss.

Modify the client to retry a few times if no response is received.

This exercise mirrors real-world constraints in UDP applications, where delivery is not guaranteed and timing matters.

Whether you're writing diagnostics tools, real-time systems, file transfer utilities, or distributed services, the ability to use raw TCP and UDP sockets gives your software direct access to communication infrastructure. Rust ensures that even at this low level, you work with strong types, explicit error handling, and memory safety.

You don't lose power or performance by choosing Rust—you gain clarity, correctness, and confidence in your network code.

Concurrent Servers with Tokio

Writing a server that can handle multiple client connections at once is a major leap in building responsive, real-world systems software. Traditional blocking I/O requires you to either spawn threads or use process-level concurrency. This works—but it's heavy, inefficient, and hard to scale beyond a few hundred connections.

Rust offers a more scalable and modern approach: **asynchronous I/O**. With **Tokio**, an asynchronous runtime built for Rust, you can write highly concurrent TCP servers that handle thousands of connections using just a handful of OS threads. Tokio uses cooperative multitasking under the hood, with Rust's `async` and `await` syntax driving the event loop.

Setting Up Tokio in Your Project

To get started with Tokio, add this to your `Cargo.toml`:

```
[dependencies]
tokio = { version = "1.37", features = ["full"] }
```

The `full` feature enables everything we need: TCP, file I/O, timers, and task spawning.

Now create a new Rust file or binary, and annotate the `main` function with `#[tokio::main]`. This macro sets up the Tokio runtime behind the scenes.

A Minimal Async TCP Server

Let's build a simple echo server. It accepts multiple TCP clients, reads incoming messages, and sends them back. Each client is handled concurrently with `tokio::spawn`.

```rust
use tokio::net::TcpListener;
use tokio::io::{AsyncReadExt, AsyncWriteExt};

#[tokio::main]
async fn main() -> tokio::io::Result<()> {
    let listener =
TcpListener::bind("127.0.0.1:8000").await?;
    println!("Server listening on 127.0.0.1:8000");

    loop {
        let (mut socket, addr) =
listener.accept().await?;
        println!("New connection from {}", addr);

        tokio::spawn(async move {
            let mut buffer = [0u8; 1024];

            loop {
                match socket.read(&mut
buffer).await {
                    Ok(0) => {
                        println!("Connection
closed: {}", addr);
                        return;
                    }
                    Ok(n) => {
                        if
socket.write_all(&buffer[..n]).await.is_err() {
                            println!("Failed to
respond to {}", addr);
                            return;
                        }
                    }
                    Err(e) => {
                        println!("Error on
connection with {}: {}", addr, e);
                        return;
                    }
```

```
                }
              }
          });
      }
}
```

Here's what's happening:

`TcpListener::bind()` starts the server.

`listener.accept()` waits for a new client.

`tokio::spawn` launches a new task for each client without blocking the main loop.

`read()` and `write_all()` are non-blocking and work only inside an `async` `fn`.

Each client is fully isolated and handled independently, but without creating new OS threads.

Shared State Across Tasks

A common use case in concurrent servers is managing shared state—like a list of connected clients or a shared database connection. You must use thread-safe containers like `Arc` and `tokio::sync::Mutex` to coordinate access safely across async tasks.

Let's create a server that:

Accepts clients

Reads a line of input

Stores it in a shared `Vec<String>`

Responds with the number of total messages seen

```
use std::sync::Arc;
use tokio::net::TcpListener;
use tokio::io::{AsyncBufReadExt, AsyncWriteExt,
BufReader};
use tokio::sync::Mutex;
```

```rust
#[tokio::main]
async fn main() -> tokio::io::Result<()> {
    let listener =
TcpListener::bind("127.0.0.1:9000").await?;
    let shared_messages =
Arc::new(Mutex::new(Vec::new()));

    loop {
        let (socket, addr) =
listener.accept().await?;
        let state = shared_messages.clone();

        tokio::spawn(async move {
            let mut reader =
BufReader::new(socket);
            let mut line = String::new();

            loop {
                line.clear();
                let bytes = reader.read_line(&mut
line).await;

                match bytes {
                    Ok(0) => {
                        println!("Client
disconnected: {}", addr);
                        break;
                    }
                    Ok(_) => {
                        let mut store =
state.lock().await;

store.push(line.trim().to_string());

                        let reply =
format!("Stored. Total messages: {}\n",
store.len());
                        if let Err(e) =
reader.get_mut().write_all(reply.as_bytes()).await
{
                            println!("Failed to
write to client: {}", e);
```

```
                                 break;
                            }
                        }
                    Err(e) => {
                        println!("Error reading
from client: {}", e);
                        break;
                    }
                }
            }
        });
    }
}
```

This server:

Buffers incoming input using `BufReader`

Uses a `tokio::sync::Mutex` for shared access

Sends back the current message count to each client

Because `Mutex` in Tokio is async-aware, it does not block the runtime like a regular thread-based mutex would.

Shutdown and Timeout Handling

Real servers need timeouts and shutdown logic. Here's how you can add a timeout to each client using `tokio::time::timeout`:

```
use tokio::time::{timeout, Duration};

let result = timeout(Duration::from_secs(10),
socket.read(&mut buffer)).await;

match result {
    Ok(Ok(n)) => { /* proceed */ }
    Ok(Err(e)) => eprintln!("Read error: {}", e),
    Err(_) => {
        eprintln!("Timeout");
        return;
    }
}
```

This pattern prevents idle clients from consuming resources forever. You can also use `tokio::signal` to listen for Ctrl+C and gracefully exit the server loop.

Exercise: Build a Multi-Client Broadcast Server

Create a server that:

Accepts multiple clients

Reads lines from each client

Broadcasts the message to all other connected clients

Use:

`Arc<Mutex<Vec<Sender>>>` where each `Sender` is a `tokio::sync::mpsc::Sender<String>`

Each client receives messages on a `Receiver` and writes them back to its socket

This structure mimics a chat server and introduces you to channel-based communication across async tasks.

Writing concurrent servers used to be hard. You had to manage threads, shared memory, blocking I/O, and synchronization all at once. Rust, with Tokio, flips that equation. You write clear, readable code using `async/await`, but you're running scalable, non-blocking infrastructure under the hood.

Writing Secure Protocols and Handling Errors

When you build software that communicates over the network, you're stepping into an environment where anything can happen. Clients may send malformed input, attackers may craft deliberately malicious messages, and legitimate users may disconnect without warning. A secure and reliable networked system must be able to handle all of this—gracefully, predictably, and defensively.

Security starts with **control over how input is interpreted**, continues with **careful validation of protocol state and boundaries**, and is supported by

precise and structured error handling. Rust gives you strong tools to do all of this. Its strict typing, safe memory model, and powerful error-handling mechanisms make it easier to write secure, correct protocol code without relying on undefined behavior, buffer overflows, or guesswork.

Designing a Simple Line-Based Protocol

Let's begin with a basic protocol that's line-oriented: clients send newline-terminated commands like PING\n, and the server responds with well-formed replies like PONG\n.

This kind of text-based protocol is easy to test and extend. But it's also the most commonly abused—because parsing strings is error-prone when not handled carefully.

Let's define a minimal protocol parser:

```
fn parse_command(line: &str) -> Result<&'static
str, &'static str> {
    match line.trim_end() {
        "PING" => Ok("PONG\n"),
        "HELLO" => Ok("WELCOME\n"),
        _ => Err("ERROR Unknown Command\n"),
    }
}
```

Notice that we trim only the end (trim_end()), because we expect \n at the end. We never assume the string is valid beyond what we've checked.

Here's how you integrate this into an async TCP server using Tokio:

```
use tokio::net::TcpListener;
use tokio::io::{AsyncBufReadExt, AsyncWriteExt,
BufReader};

#[tokio::main]
async fn main() -> tokio::io::Result<()> {
    let listener =
TcpListener::bind("127.0.0.1:8000").await?;
    println!("Secure protocol server running on
port 8000");

    loop {
```

117

```rust
        let (socket, addr) =
listener.accept().await?;
        println!("Client connected: {}", addr);

        tokio::spawn(async move {
            let mut reader =
BufReader::new(socket);
            let mut line = String::new();

            loop {
                line.clear();
                let read = match
reader.read_line(&mut line).await {
                    Ok(0) => {
                        println!("Connection closed
by client: {}", addr);
                        break;
                    }
                    Ok(n) => n,
                    Err(e) => {
                        eprintln!("Error reading
from {}: {}", addr, e);
                        break;
                    }
                };

                let response = match
parse_command(&line) {
                    Ok(reply) => reply,
                    Err(err) => err,
                };

                if let Err(e) =
reader.get_mut().write_all(response.as_bytes()).awa
it {
                    eprintln!("Failed to write to
{}: {}", addr, e);
                    break;
                }
            }
        });
    }
```

```
}
```

This server:

Reads line-by-line

Parses each command safely

Responds predictably

Handles disconnects and I/O errors

That's the baseline: a secure protocol starts by **not assuming the client will behave correctly**.

Preventing Protocol Abuse

Let's think defensively.

Limit input size. Don't allow unbounded reads from the client. Use a buffer with a max size.

Reject invalid UTF-8. If you read raw bytes (e.g., in a binary protocol), don't use `from_utf8_lossy`. Validate first, or use a format like `bincode`.

Check command length before parsing.

Update your parser to prevent command injection or denial of service:

```
fn parse_command(line: &str) -> Result<&'static
str, &'static str> {
    if line.len() > 100 {
        return Err("ERROR Command Too Long\n");
    }

    match line.trim_end() {
        "PING" => Ok("PONG\n"),
        "HELLO" => Ok("WELCOME\n"),
        _ => Err("ERROR Unknown Command\n"),
    }
}
```

You can also guard against too many requests per connection by counting requests and terminating if a limit is reached.

Handling Binary Protocols with Length Prefixes

Many protocols use **length-prefixed frames** instead of newline-terminated strings. This works well for binary formats.

Here's how you'd read a framed message:

```rust
use tokio::io::{AsyncReadExt, AsyncWriteExt};
use tokio::net::TcpStream;

async fn handle_framed(mut stream: TcpStream) ->
tokio::io::Result<()> {
    loop {
        let mut length_buf = [0u8; 4];

        if stream.read_exact(&mut
length_buf).await.is_err() {
            break;
        }

        let length =
u32::from_be_bytes(length_buf);

        if length > 1024 {
            stream.write_all(b"ERR Too
Long\n").await?;
            break;
        }

        let mut payload = vec![0u8; length as
usize];
        if stream.read_exact(&mut
payload).await.is_err() {
            break;
        }

        // In a real server, you'd deserialize or
process this safely.
        stream.write_all(b"ACK\n").await?;
    }

    Ok(())
}
```

This prevents buffer overruns by:

Reading a 4-byte length field

Rejecting overly long messages

Allocating only what's needed

This structure is the basis of many real-world protocols, from gRPC to Redis.

Using Structured Errors with `thiserror` or `anyhow`

Rust makes error handling structured, not silent. Use custom error types to describe what failed and why.

```
[dependencies]
thiserror = "1.0"
use thiserror::Error;

#[derive(Error, Debug)]
pub enum ProtocolError {
    #[error("Command too long")]
    TooLong,
    #[error("Invalid command")]
    Invalid,
    #[error("I/O error: {0}")]
    Io(#[from] std::io::Error),
}
```

Now your command parser or handler can return `Result<_, ProtocolError>`, and you can `match` on exact failure causes.

Exercise: Build a Command Whitelist Server

Write a server that:

Accepts TCP connections

Receives lines from clients

Only accepts one of: `HELLO`, `PING`, or `BYE`

Tracks how many commands each client sends

Disconnects any client that sends an invalid command or sends more than 5 total commands

You should:

Use a per-connection command counter

Define a parser that strictly checks command format

Send back explicit ERROR responses for each rejection reason

This exercise mimics how real application servers enforce policies, limits, and consistent behavior under pressure.

Protocol security is not a feature—it's the foundation of every networked system that works reliably and safely in the real world. Rust doesn't guess or assume anything about your input. It makes you handle errors, define boundaries, and write predictable state transitions explicitly.

By applying:

Careful parsing strategies

Proper error handling

Input length limits

Validations before usage

—you're writing software that can be trusted to stay up under real traffic, withstand probing or abuse, and serve valid clients correctly.

Chapter 8: Embedded and Bare-Metal Rust

Writing code for embedded systems means you're no longer programming *with* an operating system—you're writing code that often *is* the operating system, or at least part of the firmware that talks directly to the hardware. There's no file system, no standard output, no memory allocator. In many cases, there's not even a main function in the traditional sense.

Rust is extremely well-suited for this level of systems programming. It gives you memory safety, zero-cost abstractions, and precise control over every byte. But to use it effectively in these environments, you need to understand how to work without the standard library, how to interface directly with registers and peripherals, and how to design firmware that can live at the lowest levels of computing hardware.

Working in `no_std` Environments

When you write embedded or bare-metal software, you're working without the comforts of an operating system. There's no file system, no network stack, no threads, and—critically—no standard library. The `std` crate depends on OS services like memory allocation and file descriptors. In embedded systems, those services simply don't exist. That's where Rust's `no_std` environment comes into play.

Rust makes this explicit and safe. You tell the compiler you're writing code for a system that doesn't support `std`, and it compiles only what's possible in that context. This gives you maximum control, minimal overhead, and the opportunity to use Rust in truly constrained environments—such as microcontrollers, soft-core CPUs, or bootloaders.

Declaring #![no_std]

To begin writing a `no_std` application, your crate must explicitly opt out of the standard library.

At the top of your `main.rs` or `lib.rs`, write:

```
#![no_std]
```

```
#![no_main]
```

`#![no_std]` tells the compiler to exclude the standard library and instead link to `core`—a minimal library with essentials like `Option`, `Result`, and `Iterator`.

`#![no_main]` means you won't use Rust's usual `fn main()` entry point. You'll provide your own, either through a runtime crate or manually.

In embedded projects, `main()` is often replaced with a device-specific entry function provided by a crate like `cortex-m-rt`, `riscv-rt`, or a board-specific runtime.

For example, if you're using an ARM Cortex-M microcontroller, your main function might look like this:

```
use cortex_m_rt::entry;

#[entry]
fn main() -> ! {
    // Your startup code here
    loop {
        // Embedded programs usually run forever
    }
}
```

The return type `!` means this function never returns, which is appropriate for firmware that runs until powered off.

Handling Panics Without `std`

In a full system, panic! would print an error message and unwind the stack. In `no_std`, there's no such mechanism. You must define your own panic behavior.

There are two common strategies:

1. Abort on panic:

Use the `panic-halt` crate, which simply enters an infinite loop when a panic occurs.

```
[dependencies]
```

```
panic-halt = "0.2"

use panic_halt as _; // Set the panic handler
```

2. Custom panic handler:

If you want to log the panic somewhere (e.g. over UART), define your own
panic handler:

```
use core::panic::PanicInfo;

#[panic_handler]
fn panic(_info: &PanicInfo) -> ! {
    // Log message or blink LED here
    loop {}
}
```

Your handler receives information about the file and line number where the
panic occurred. You can use this to signal a fault condition to the user or halt
the system for debugging.

Setting Up the Target and Toolchain

When building for embedded systems, you need a **cross-compilation target**.
For example, for a Cortex-M4 chip:

rustup target add thumbv7em-none-eabihf

Your `Cargo.toml` might include:

```
[profile.release]

codegen-units = 1

lto = true

debug = true
```

Then build with:

cargo build --release --target=thumbv7em-none-eabihf

This produces a `.elf` file you can flash to your board using `probe-rs`, `cargo-
embed`, or a vendor tool.

Using `core` and Avoiding Allocation

Without `std`, you don't get things like `Vec`, `String`, or heap allocation by default. Instead, you use `core`, which includes:

Basic types: `Option`, `Result`, `bool`, integers, floats

Traits: `Copy`, `Clone`, `Iterator`, `Add`, `Eq`, `Ord`

Functional tools: `map`, `and_then`, `unwrap_or`, etc.

Formatting macros (via `core::fmt`)

You can build powerful programs even in this minimal environment. If you need dynamic memory, you can use an allocator like `alloc-cortex-m` or implement a bump allocator of your own, but most embedded applications are designed to avoid the heap entirely.

For string formatting, `core::fmt` lets you implement `Display` and format values into fixed-size buffers.

Example: formatting into a static buffer

```
use core::fmt::Write;

struct Logger;

impl Write for Logger {
    fn write_str(&mut self, s: &str) ->
core::fmt::Result {
        // Send s over serial, etc.
        Ok(())
    }
}

fn log_status(code: u8) {
    let mut logger = Logger;
    writeln!(&mut logger, "Status: {}", code).ok();
}
```

Using Board Support Crates and Runtimes

Most embedded Rust development uses **board support crates (BSCs)** and **hardware abstraction layers (HALs)**, which wrap device-specific details behind portable APIs.

For example, a typical `Cargo.toml` for an STM32 board might include:

```
[dependencies]

cortex-m = "0.7"

cortex-m-rt = "0.7"

stm32f4xx-hal = { version = "0.17", features =
["stm32f401", "rt"] }

panic-halt = "0.2"
```

The `rt` feature includes the startup code and interrupt vector table.

A minimal blinking LED program:

```
#![no_std]
#![no_main]

use cortex_m_rt::entry;
use panic_halt as _;
use stm32f4xx_hal::{pac, prelude::*, delay::Delay};

#[entry]
fn main() -> ! {
    let dp = pac::Peripherals::take().unwrap();
    let rcc = dp.RCC.constrain();
    let clocks =
rcc.cfgr.sysclk(48.mhz()).freeze();

    let gpioc = dp.GPIOC.split();
    let mut led =
gpioc.pc13.into_push_pull_output();

    let mut delay =
Delay::new(cortex_m::Peripherals::take().unwrap().S
YST, clocks);
```

```
loop {
    led.set_high();
    delay.delay_ms(500u16);
    led.set_low();
    delay.delay_ms(500u16);
}
}
```

This works entirely without `std`, but uses the full power of Rust's type system and safety guarantees to control real hardware.

Exercise: Write a no_std LED Blink Loop

Target: any Cortex-M board (e.g. STM32F103, STM32F4, nRF52)

Steps:

Use `#![no_std]` and `#![no_main]`

Set up a timer using the HAL crate

Toggle a GPIO pin in an infinite loop

Use a `panic_halt` strategy

Build for your chip's target using `cargo build --target ...`

Flash with `cargo-embed` or `probe-rs`

If you're running in QEMU or a simulator, use `semihosting` to debug output through the host console.

Working in `no_std` mode changes how you think about software. You don't rely on dynamic allocation, external services, or OS support. Every part of your program is under your control—compiled for a specific chip, linked to specific memory addresses, and started from the first instruction after power-on.

Rust gives you the control and safety you need to write firmware and low-level systems code that is:

Small and deterministic

Safe from common pointer errors

Easy to reason about at both the byte and logic level

You're not just compiling a program—you're building something that runs on bare silicon. And Rust is built for that.

Interacting with Hardware

When you're working in embedded Rust, interacting with hardware means writing code that communicates directly with the peripherals built into your microcontroller—things like timers, GPIO, serial interfaces, and buses like I²C or SPI. At this level, there is no operating system between your code and the hardware. You're reading and writing directly to memory-mapped registers that control pins, clocks, and communication protocols.

Rust gives you the safety and precision to do this with confidence. You can write code that manipulates these low-level registers safely, with full type checking and no undefined behavior. And with the help of **Hardware Abstraction Layers (HALs)** and **Peripheral Access Crates (PACs)**, you can do this in a way that is reusable and portable across different boards and chip families.

Memory-Mapped Registers

Every peripheral in a microcontroller is controlled through **memory-mapped registers**—specific memory addresses that control hardware behavior. These registers are located at known addresses in memory, which are documented in the chip's reference manual.

To interact with them in Rust, you convert these addresses into raw pointers and use `core::ptr::read_volatile()` or `write_volatile()`.

Here's an example writing to a GPIO register directly:

```
#![no_std]
#![no_main]

use core::ptr;

#[no_mangle]
pub extern "C" fn main() -> ! {
    const GPIOC_MODER: *mut u32 = 0x4800_0800 as
*mut u32; // GPIOC_MODER
```

```rust
    const GPIOC_ODR: *mut u32 = 0x4800_0814 as *mut
u32;    // GPIOC_ODR

    unsafe {
        // Set pin PC13 as output (01)
        let moder =
ptr::read_volatile(GPIOC_MODER);
        ptr::write_volatile(GPIOC_MODER, (moder &
!(0b11 << 26)) | (0b01 << 26));

        // Toggle PC13 in a loop
        loop {
            ptr::write_volatile(GPIOC_ODR, 1 <<
13);
            delay();
            ptr::write_volatile(GPIOC_ODR, 0);
            delay();
        }
    }
}

fn delay() {
    for _ in 0..1_000_000 {
        unsafe { core::arch::asm!("nop") }
    }
}
```

This is completely valid, direct register-level programming. It's unsafe—but only in a narrowly defined, controlled way.

Using Peripheral Access Crates (PACs)

Writing directly to hardcoded addresses is risky and tedious. Instead, we use **PACs**—crates auto-generated from SVD files (provided by chip vendors) that define all registers, fields, and bits in a structured way.

For example, to use STM32F4 peripherals:

```toml
[dependencies]

stm32f4 = "0.15.1"

cortex-m-rt = "0.7"
```

130

```
panic-halt = "0.2"
```

Now in your code:

```
#![no_std]
#![no_main]

use cortex_m_rt::entry;
use panic_halt as _;
use stm32f4::stm32f401;

#[entry]
fn main() -> ! {
    let dp =
stm32f401::Peripherals::take().unwrap();

    let rcc = &dp.RCC;
    let gpioa = &dp.GPIOA;

    // Enable GPIOA clock
    rcc.ahb1enr.modify(|_, w|
w.gpioaen().enabled());

    // Set PA5 as output
    gpioa.moder.modify(|_, w| w.moder5().output());

    loop {
        gpioa.odr.modify(|_, w|
w.odr5().set_bit());
        delay();
        gpioa.odr.modify(|_, w|
w.odr5().clear_bit());
        delay();
    }
}

fn delay() {
    for _ in 0..100_000 {
        unsafe { core::arch::asm!("nop") }
    }
}
```

This approach:

Uses typed register access instead of raw pointers

Ensures only valid register values can be written

Clearly communicates hardware intent

Working with a Hardware Abstraction Layer (HAL)

PACs give you control, but they can be verbose. A **HAL** builds on top of PACs to offer safer, simpler APIs.

Here's how you might toggle an LED with the `stm32f4xx-hal` crate:

```
[dependencies]
stm32f4xx-hal = { version = "0.17", features =
["stm32f401", "rt"] }
cortex-m-rt = "0.7"
panic-halt = "0.2"
#![no_std]
#![no_main]

use cortex_m_rt::entry;
use panic_halt as _;
use stm32f4xx_hal::{prelude::*, stm32};

#[entry]
fn main() -> ! {
    let dp = stm32::Peripherals::take().unwrap();

    let rcc = dp.RCC.constrain();
    let clocks = rcc.cfgr.freeze();

    let gpioa = dp.GPIOA.split();
    let mut led =
gpioa.pa5.into_push_pull_output();

    loop {
        led.set_high().unwrap();
        delay();
        led.set_low().unwrap();
        delay();
    }
}
```

```
fn delay() {
    for _ in 0..100_000 {
        unsafe { core::arch::asm!("nop") }
    }
}
```

This version uses Rust traits like `OutputPin` and provides runtime-checked I/O access without needing to track every bitfield manually.

Interacting with Other Peripherals

Let's briefly touch on using a timer and UART.

Timer example: blinking with a delay

```
use stm32f4xx_hal::{delay::Delay, prelude::*,
stm32};

let cp = cortex_m::Peripherals::take().unwrap();
let dp = stm32::Peripherals::take().unwrap();

let rcc = dp.RCC.constrain();
let clocks = rcc.cfgr.freeze();

let mut delay = Delay::new(cp.SYST, clocks);
delay.delay_ms(1000_u32);
```

UART example: writing to a serial port

```
use stm32f4xx_hal::{serial::config::Config,
serial::Serial};

let gpioa = dp.GPIOA.split();
let tx = gpioa.pa2.into_alternate();
let rx = gpioa.pa3.into_alternate();

let serial = Serial::usart2(dp.USART2, (tx, rx),
Config::default(), clocks).unwrap();
let (mut tx, _rx) = serial.split();

use core::fmt::Write;
writeln!(tx, "Hello, world!\r").ok();
```

This demonstrates:

Using HAL to configure USART

Sending text over serial

Formatting output using `core::fmt::Write`

You can connect this to a serial terminal to log messages, debug sensors, or send commands.

Exercise: Toggle a Pin Based on Button Press

Create a firmware app that:

Configures one pin as input (with pull-up)

Configures another pin as output

Polls the input in a loop

When pressed (low), sets the output high

Use only HAL functions, no raw register access. Try running it on real hardware or QEMU simulation.

This will teach you how to interact with inputs and outputs at the hardware level using safe APIs.

Talking to hardware in Rust doesn't mean writing unsafe pointer math all day. You can do that when needed—but you also have access to safe, high-level abstractions that compile down to the same efficient instructions, with the added benefit of type safety, bounds checks, and strong encapsulation.

You're not guessing what bits to flip. You're writing logic that says, "Turn on the LED," "Check the sensor," or "Send this byte"—and the compiler makes sure you get it right.

Writing Drivers and Firmware

Writing drivers and firmware in Rust means taking direct responsibility for how your code interacts with hardware components—safely, predictably, and efficiently. A driver is simply code that knows how to talk to a specific piece of hardware: a sensor, display, actuator, or communication chip. Firmware is the full application logic that includes drivers, control flow, and possibly interrupt or timer-based behavior. When you build both with Rust, you're not only in control of the machine—you're doing so with the added assurance of strong type checking and memory safety, without sacrificing performance.

Designing a Hardware Driver with `embedded-hal`

To keep drivers portable and reusable, embedded Rust developers typically build on the `embedded-hal` crate. It defines a set of traits for common peripherals—GPIO, I2C, SPI, serial, timers, PWM, and more—so your driver can work with any microcontroller that implements these traits.

Here's how to write a simple driver for a hypothetical I2C temperature sensor.

First, add the necessary dependencies to your `Cargo.toml`:

[dependencies]

embedded-hal = "1.0.0"

Now define the driver:

```
use embedded_hal::i2c::{I2c, Error};

pub struct TempSensor<I2C> {
    i2c: I2C,
    address: u8,
}

impl<I2C, E> TempSensor<I2C>
where
    I2C: I2c<Error = E>,
{
    pub fn new(i2c: I2C, address: u8) -> Self {
        Self { i2c, address }
    }

    pub fn read_temp_celsius(&mut self) ->
Result<f32, E> {
        let mut buf = [0u8; 2];

        self.i2c.write_read(self.address, &[0x01],
&mut buf)?;
```

```
        let raw = u16::from_be_bytes(buf);
        Ok((raw as f32) * 0.1)
    }
}
```

This driver:

Accepts any I2C interface that implements the `embedded-hal` trait

Sends a command to read the temperature

Converts the response into a human-readable floating-point value

Because this is fully generic, it works on any microcontroller, simulated environment, or mock implementation—so long as it satisfies the `I2c` trait.

Integrating the Driver into Firmware

Now that you've written a reusable driver, you can use it in real firmware.

If you're using an STM32 board, your `Cargo.toml` might include:

```
[dependencies]

cortex-m = "0.7"

cortex-m-rt = "0.7"

stm32f4xx-hal = { version = "0.17", features =
["stm32f401", "rt"] }

embedded-hal = "1.0.0"

panic-halt = "0.2"
```

Your firmware might then look like this:

```
#![no_std]
#![no_main]

use panic_halt as _;
use cortex_m_rt::entry;
use stm32f4xx_hal::{prelude::*, stm32, i2c::I2c};
use core::fmt::Write;
```

```rust
mod tempsensor;
use tempsensor::TempSensor;

#[entry]
fn main() -> ! {
    let dp = stm32::Peripherals::take().unwrap();
    let cp =
cortex_m::Peripherals::take().unwrap();

    let rcc = dp.RCC.constrain();
    let clocks = rcc.cfgr.freeze();

    let gpiob = dp.GPIOB.split();
    let scl = gpiob.pb6.into_alternate();
    let sda = gpiob.pb7.into_alternate();

    let i2c = I2c::new(dp.I2C1, (scl, sda),
100.khz(), clocks);

    let mut sensor = TempSensor::new(i2c, 0x48);

    let gpioc = dp.GPIOC.split();
    let mut led =
gpioc.pc13.into_push_pull_output();

    let mut delay =
stm32f4xx_hal::delay::Delay::new(cp.SYST, clocks);

    loop {
        match sensor.read_temp_celsius() {
            Ok(temp) => {
                if temp > 30.0 {
                    led.set_high().ok(); // Turn on
warning LED
                } else {
                    led.set_low().ok();
                }
            }
            Err(_) => {
                led.set_high().ok(); // Turn on LED
to indicate error
            }
```

```
        }

        delay.delay_ms(1000u16);
    }
}
```

This firmware:

Initializes I2C

Instantiates the reusable driver

Polls the sensor once per second

Turns an LED on/off based on the temperature

This is a real-world pattern: sensor polling loop, driver logic, and control output based on readings.

Structuring Driver APIs for Flexibility

A well-designed driver should:

Work with any compatible hardware interface

Abstract internal protocol logic

Return clear, typed errors

Allow easy integration into firmware

To support testability and mocking, define a trait for your driver's high-level interface:

```
pub trait Thermometer {

    fn read_celsius(&mut self) -> Result<f32,
core::convert::Infallible>;

}
```

Now any type that implements this trait can be used in your firmware logic, allowing for mocking in unit tests or substituting drivers at runtime.

Building a Custom Protocol Driver (Bit-Banged)

What if you don't have I2C or SPI hardware available? You can implement drivers using GPIO "bit-banging"—manually setting pins high/low with delays.

Here's a stripped-down example using embedded-hal GPIO traits:

```rust
use embedded_hal::digital::v2::{InputPin,
OutputPin};
use embedded_hal::blocking::delay::DelayUs;

pub struct BitBangDriver<CLK, DIO, DELAY> {
    clk: CLK,
    dio: DIO,
    delay: DELAY,
}

impl<CLK, DIO, DELAY, E> BitBangDriver<CLK, DIO,
DELAY>
where
    CLK: OutputPin<Error = E>,
    DIO: OutputPin<Error = E> + InputPin<Error =
E>,
    DELAY: DelayUs<u8>,
{
    pub fn new(clk: CLK, dio: DIO, delay: DELAY) ->
Self {
        Self { clk, dio, delay }
    }

    pub fn send_bit(&mut self, bit: bool) ->
Result<(), E> {
        if bit {
            self.dio.set_high()?;
        } else {
            self.dio.set_low()?;
        }

        self.delay.delay_us(1);
        self.clk.set_high()?;
        self.delay.delay_us(1);
        self.clk.set_low()?;
        Ok(())
    }
```

}

This pattern is useful for talking to displays, WS2812 LEDs, or sensors that use proprietary protocols without hardware support.

Exercise: Build a Reusable Driver for a GPIO-Controlled Buzzer

Define a `Buzzer` struct that:

Accepts a `Pin` implementing `OutputPin`

Provides a method `beep(duration_ms: u16)`

Uses a delay provider to keep the buzzer active for that time

Use the HAL's `Delay` and toggle the pin high, wait, then low. Make sure to structure the driver to be generic over any pin and delay source.

Use this to trigger alarms or heartbeat beeps in your firmware logic.

Rust empowers you to write embedded drivers that are:

Generic and portable

Type-safe and memory-safe

Free of pointer casting or buffer overflows

Easy to integrate and test

You can reuse the same driver logic on a real board, in a simulator, or inside a unit test. You're building firmware that behaves consistently, interacts predictably with hardware, and compiles down to tight, efficient code that fits into small footprints and tight timing loops.

Chapter 9: Debugging, Testing, and Optimization

When writing embedded systems in Rust, correctness is not optional. You're often working with hardware that lacks guardrails. A mistake might mean a peripheral silently fails to initialize, a timing-sensitive task misses its window, or worse—your device resets unexpectedly without any output. That's why robust **debugging**, **testing**, and **performance optimization** aren't afterthoughts—they're part of your design loop.

Rust gives you a unique advantage in this space. Because its type system prevents many classes of bugs at compile time, you start with a more reliable foundation. But correctness goes beyond types. Embedded systems must also be **observable**, **testable**, and **tuned**—especially when running without an operating system, where traditional logs and tools are unavailable or limited.

Writing Reliable Tests and Property Checks

Writing embedded firmware is not just about making things work once. It's about making sure they *always* work—on every board, in every condition, for every edge case you didn't think of during development. That's where testing becomes essential.

Rust gives you a powerful testing framework that you can use to validate your code logic—even when that code will eventually run in a `no_std`, bare-metal context. The secret is to structure your logic so that it's testable on your development machine, and only the hardware-specific parts are isolated behind interfaces or traits. You don't test hardware with `cargo test`, but you absolutely *can* test the control logic, data parsing, protocol handling, and driver interactions that make your firmware work correctly.

Start with Unit Tests on Logic You Control

The easiest place to begin testing is in pure logic: no hardware, no side effects. If you have a function that parses command bytes, translates ADC readings to voltage, or processes a sensor value, you can write a unit test right next to it.

Here's a function that converts a raw ADC value into millivolts for a 12-bit ADC and 3.3V reference:

```rust
pub fn adc_to_millivolts(raw: u16) -> u32 {
    (raw as u32 * 3300) / 4095
}
```
Now let's test it:
```rust
#[cfg(test)]
mod tests {
    use super::*;

    #[test]
    fn test_adc_zero() {
        assert_eq!(adc_to_millivolts(0), 0);
    }

    #[test]
    fn test_adc_max() {
        assert_eq!(adc_to_millivolts(4095), 3300);
    }

    #[test]
    fn test_midpoint() {
        assert_eq!(adc_to_millivolts(2048), 1650);
    }
}
```

You can run these tests with `cargo test`, and they'll execute on your development machine, not the embedded target. These are fast, reliable, and reproducible—everything you want in early-stage validation.

Isolate Hardware with Traits for Easy Mocking

Real embedded programs deal with hardware. But if you hardcode the hardware access into your logic, you can't test it easily. So you write **interfaces**—traits in Rust—that describe how your logic talks to the hardware.

Let's define a trait for a temperature sensor:

```rust
pub trait Thermometer {

    fn read_celsius(&mut self) -> Result<f32, ()>;

}
```

Now write a firmware module that blinks an LED if the temperature is over a threshold:

```
pub fn check_temp<T: Thermometer>(sensor: &mut T) -
> bool {

    match sensor.read_celsius() {

        Ok(temp) => temp > 30.0,

        Err(_) => false,

    }

}
```

To test it:

```
#[cfg(test)]
mod tests {
    use super::*;

    struct FakeSensor(f32);
    impl Thermometer for FakeSensor {
        fn read_celsius(&mut self) -> Result<f32,
()> {
            Ok(self.0)
        }
    }

    #[test]
    fn test_temp_high() {
        let mut s = FakeSensor(35.0);
        assert_eq!(check_temp(&mut s), true);
    }

    #[test]
    fn test_temp_low() {
        let mut s = FakeSensor(25.0);
        assert_eq!(check_temp(&mut s), false);
    }
}
```

This test is fast, runs locally, and tests real decision logic. You're no longer guessing whether your firmware will work—you've proved it with data.

Use Property-Based Testing for Broader Coverage

Let's say you want to test that any temperature above 30 turns the fan on. Instead of picking three values and testing them by hand, you can **generate hundreds of values automatically** and assert that the logic always behaves correctly.

Rust's `proptest` crate does exactly that.

First, add it to `Cargo.toml`:

[dev-dependencies]

proptest = "1"

Then write a property-based test:

```
use proptest::prelude::*;

fn should_run_fan(temp: f32) -> bool {
    temp > 30.0
}

proptest! {
    #[test]
    fn fan_on_if_temp_exceeds_threshold(temp in
30.1f32..=100.0) {
        prop_assert!(should_run_fan(temp));
    }

    #[test]
    fn fan_off_below_threshold(temp in -
40.0f32..=30.0) {
        prop_assert!(!should_run_fan(temp));
    }
}
```

Now every time you run `cargo test`, proptest generates hundreds of random inputs within the specified range and checks the assertions. If a test fails, proptest finds the smallest failing example and prints it out for you.

This approach is excellent for testing:

Data parsers (e.g., "this packet is never longer than 64 bytes")

State machines ("this state always leads to a valid transition")

Checksums ("computed CRC always matches the input")

Testing Error Handling and Fallbacks

A well-behaved firmware doesn't just work—it handles failure without crashing. So test the edge cases.

Here's a test that ensures a fallback is used if sensor reading fails:

```
struct BrokenSensor;
impl Thermometer for BrokenSensor {
    fn read_celsius(&mut self) -> Result<f32, ()> {
        Err(())
    }
}

#[test]
fn test_fallback_on_error() {
    let mut sensor = BrokenSensor;
    assert_eq!(check_temp(&mut sensor), false); //
No panic
}
```

When your firmware logic handles the full range of inputs, including timeouts, dropped packets, and hardware faults, your device becomes predictable and robust—even under stress.

Exercise: Write and Test a Packet Parser

Define a function that accepts a [u8; 5] packet:

First byte is a command

Last 4 bytes are a big-endian u32 payload

Write a function that returns (u8, u32)

Write unit tests for:

A normal command and payload

The maximum payload

All zeros

Use `proptest` to generate hundreds of random byte arrays and assert that the function never panics

This gives you experience in writing logic that interprets raw bytes—a critical skill for drivers, protocols, and low-level firmware systems.

Testing embedded Rust code is not about mocking everything or building huge frameworks. It's about isolating the logic that *can* be tested off-device, and making sure it behaves consistently across all possible inputs.

Rust gives you the structure, the types, and the tooling to do this with precision:

Use `#[cfg(test)]` and write logic-first tests

Build abstractions over hardware using traits

Use property testing to expose the gaps in your thinking

Validate not just correctness, but robustness

This is how you build embedded firmware that's resilient in production, not just functional in the lab.

Using Profilers, Debuggers, and Static Analysis Tools

Writing embedded firmware in Rust gives you confidence that your code is memory-safe and type-correct—but it doesn't mean the system will always behave correctly once it's running on hardware. Once your firmware compiles and runs, you need visibility into what it's doing. You need to inspect it at runtime, monitor its memory and CPU behavior, and analyze it for inefficiencies or flaws that aren't obvious in the code.

This is where **profilers**, **debuggers**, and **static analysis tools** come in. These are your eyes and ears when you're working on real hardware—tools that tell you what your firmware is doing, how well it's performing, and where it might be going wrong.

In embedded systems, debugging can't rely on print statements. You might not even have a display or serial output. Instead, you rely on **debug probes**, **RTT logging**, **breakpoints**, and **symbol inspection** to diagnose behavior on the fly. Rust integrates well with these tools. You can pause the CPU, inspect memory, view backtraces, or even live-log data with minimal overhead.

Debugging Embedded Rust with GDB and `probe-rs`

To debug Rust code running on a microcontroller, you typically connect a **debug probe**—like an ST-Link, J-Link, or CMSIS-DAP adapter—and use GDB (the GNU debugger) to interface with it.

Step 1: Build your firmware with debug info

In your `Cargo.toml`, ensure this is set:

```
[profile.dev]

debug = true
```

And compile your firmware for the correct target:

```
cargo build --target thumbv7em-none-eabihf
```

This produces a `.elf` file with symbol information.

Step 2: Start a GDB session

Install the required tools:

```
rustup component add llvm-tools-preview

cargo install cargo-binutils
```

Start GDB:

```
gdb-multiarch target/thumbv7em-none-
eabihf/debug/your_firmware
```

Connect to the target with OpenOCD or `probe-rs` running in a separate terminal, or use `probe-run` to streamline the process.

Inside GDB:

```
target remote :3333
```

```
load
```

```
break main
```

```
continue
```

This loads your firmware onto the device, sets a breakpoint at `main`, and continues execution. You can inspect registers, memory, and variable values:

```
info registers
```

```
x/32x 0x2000_0000
```

```
print my_variable
```

```
backtrace
```

This is essential for diagnosing unexpected behavior like lockups, faults, or uninitialized state.

Real-Time Logging with `defmt` and RTT

RTT (Real-Time Transfer) is a mechanism for logging messages from an embedded target using the debug probe—not UART. This means no pins are used and it works even when interrupts are off.

Set up your project with `defmt`:

```
[dependencies]
defmt = "0.3"
defmt-rtt = "0.3"
panic-probe = "0.3"


[features]
default = ["defmt-default"]
```

Add to your `main.rs`:

```
use defmt_rtt as _;
use panic_probe as _;

#[entry]
fn main() -> ! {
    defmt::info!("System initialized");
    loop {
        defmt::warn!("tick");
    }
}
```

Flash and monitor with `probe-run`:

```
cargo install probe-run
```

```
cargo run --release
```

This logs over RTT with virtually no performance impact and integrates with `defmt` formatting macros. You can use `defmt::debug!`, `defmt::info!`, or `defmt::error!` just like traditional logging systems.

Static Analysis with Clippy

Rust's `clippy` tool scans your code for common mistakes, inefficiencies, and non-idiomatic patterns. It catches bugs that aren't always syntactic errors.

Install it:

```
rustup component add clippy
```

Run it on your embedded crate:

```
cargo clippy --target=thumbv7em-none-eabihf
```

Clippy will flag:

Missing `.await` in async code

Unused results

Manual implementations of things that `derive` could solve

Arithmetic that might overflow

149

Inefficient clone or borrow patterns

For embedded development, this is especially helpful in catching operations that may silently waste CPU cycles or stack space.

Inspecting Binary Size and Layout

Embedded targets often have strict limits: 128KB of flash, 32KB of RAM, or less. To stay within those boundaries, you need to understand what's consuming space.

Install `cargo-binutils`:

```
cargo install cargo-binutils
```

Check binary size:

```
cargo size --target thumbv7em-none-eabihf --release
-- -A
```

This shows section sizes:

text	data	bss	dec	hex
12084	64	1024	13172	3374

Disassemble your binary:

```
cargo objdump --target thumbv7em-none-eabihf --
release -- --disassemble
```

You can trace through your compiled functions and see whether the compiler is inlining effectively, or whether loops are using unrolled logic that's too large.

You can also use cargo-bloat to break down size by function or crate.

```
cargo install cargo-bloat
cargo bloat --release --target thumbv7em-none-
eabihf
```

This is extremely helpful when optimizing a large firmware image for flash constraints.

Memory Inspection and Fault Debugging

Rust panics are silent by default in `no_std`. To help with diagnosis, enable a panic handler that logs fault info:

```
use core::panic::PanicInfo;
use defmt_rtt as _;
use panic_probe as _;

#[panic_handler]
fn panic(info: &PanicInfo) -> ! {
    defmt::error!("PANIC: {}", info);
    loop {}
}
```

If you encounter hard faults (e.g. on null dereference or invalid instruction), inspect SCB registers using `cortex-m`:

```
use cortex_m::peripheral::SCB;

let hfsr = SCB::borrow_unchecked(|scb|
scb.hfsr.read());
defmt::info!("Hard fault status: {=u32}", hfsr);
```

Pair this with GDB backtrace and RTT logs for full visibility.

Exercise: Debug a Faulty Sensor Read

Write firmware that reads from a sensor over I2C.

Intentionally configure the wrong address.

Use `defmt` to log success/failure of each transaction.

Flash the firmware and observe the output.

Set a breakpoint in GDB on the failure path and inspect memory.

You'll learn how to correlate logs with live inspection and track down silent bugs caused by misconfiguration or electrical faults.

Debugging firmware is not about guesswork. It's about tools, visibility, and discipline. Rust doesn't stop you from making logic errors—but it gives you the best tools to *find* and *understand* those errors when they happen.

Identifying and Fixing Performance Bottlenecks

In embedded systems, performance is not an afterthought—it is a design constraint. You may be dealing with strict CPU budgets, limited memory, or timing-sensitive peripherals that must be serviced at regular intervals. A firmware that runs but consumes 80% of the processor or misses deadlines under load is not viable in production. That's why finding and fixing performance bottlenecks is a crucial step in the development of robust embedded systems.

Rust gives you fine-grained control over memory layout, data movement, and execution patterns. But even with safe code, you can still run into inefficiencies—unnecessary copying, excessive dynamic dispatch, poorly placed allocations, or unoptimized control paths. Identifying these issues and addressing them systematically is how you build fast, efficient, and predictable firmware.

Measure First, Optimize Second

Optimization without measurement is guesswork. You need a concrete understanding of **where time is spent** before trying to speed things up.

Start with basic timing instrumentation using a cycle-accurate timer. On Cortex-M, the **SysTick** timer or the **DWT cycle counter** is a good place to begin.

Enable DWT:

```
use cortex_m::peripheral::DWT;



let dwt = unsafe { &*DWT::ptr() };

dwt.enable_cycle_counter();
```

Now you can time a section of code:

```
let start = DWT::get_cycle_count();

// Your function or driver here
```

```
do_something();

let end = DWT::get_cycle_count();
defmt::info!("do_something took {} cycles",
end.wrapping_sub(start));
```

This shows exactly how long a routine takes, which is critical for debugging timing-sensitive code—like bit-banged I/O, sensor sampling windows, or motor control logic.

If you're using a real-time logging crate like defmt, you can timestamp logs or measure intervals between events:

```
defmt::info!("Interrupt serviced");
```

Use these logs to profile latency in interrupt handling or driver response.

Avoid Unnecessary Heap Usage

Many microcontrollers don't have a heap, or you've explicitly disabled it using no_std. But some libraries (especially ones that use alloc) might still introduce hidden dynamic allocations.

Here's a slow pattern:

```
let mut data = Vec::new();

data.push(0x01);

data.push(0x02);
```

This allocates from the heap, and even if Vec is available, it adds unpredictable runtime cost.

Prefer fixed-size stack buffers:

```
let mut data = [0u8; 2];

data[0] = 0x01;

data[1] = 0x02;
```

153

If you're dealing with variable-length data (like UART packets), use heapless—a crate that gives you Vec, String, and Queue implementations without heap allocation:

```
use heapless::Vec;

let mut buffer: Vec<u8, 32> = Vec::new();
buffer.push(0x10).unwrap();
```

This is safe, efficient, and will not panic if you stay within bounds.

Minimize Logging and Format Overhead

Logging is helpful during development, but it can introduce serious delays if you're printing over UART or RTT, especially from interrupts.

Avoid this:

```
defmt::info!("Received frame: {:?}", data);
```

If you're logging frequently, prefer logging compact values only:

```
defmt::info!("rx_len={}", length);
```

Or disable logging in production builds:

```
[features]

default = ["defmt-logging"]

defmt-logging = []
```

And conditionally compile logs:

```
#[cfg(feature = "defmt-logging")]

defmt::info!("debug log");
```

This removes logging entirely from release firmware, reducing flash usage and CPU cycles spent on formatting.

Profile Your Event Loop and Interrupts

If your firmware uses an event loop (e.g., RTIC or bare main loop), bottlenecks can occur if any one task blocks the loop too long. Measure each stage of the loop:

```
let start = DWT::get_cycle_count();
poll_i2c();
let mid = DWT::get_cycle_count();
poll_uart();
let end = DWT::get_cycle_count();

defmt::info!("i2c={} uart={}", mid - start, end - mid);
```

You can then inspect whether any task consistently takes too long and violates deadlines.

Similarly, if your interrupt handler is doing too much work, offload processing to the main loop by setting a flag or queuing data:

```
#[interrupt]
fn USART1() {
    let byte = usart1.read().unwrap();
    buffer.enqueue(byte).ok(); // Defer processing
}
```
Then process it outside the interrupt:
```
loop {
    while let Some(b) = buffer.dequeue() {
        handle_byte(b);
    }
}
```

This keeps interrupt latency low and avoids starving time-critical tasks.

Eliminate Costly Abstractions

Rust's traits and generics are powerful, but some patterns introduce unnecessary overhead.

Avoid using `Box<dyn Trait>` in tight loops. Trait objects require dynamic dispatch and heap allocation.

Prefer generics:

```
fn handle_sensor<T: Sensor>(sensor: &mut T) {
    sensor.read();
}
```

This monomorphizes at compile time—no runtime cost, no indirection.

Also watch out for large stack frames caused by deeply nested functions or large inlined buffers. Use `cargo asm` or `cargo llvm-lines` to inspect the size of generated functions:

```
cargo install cargo-asm

cargo asm your_crate::your_function
```

And use `.iter().copied().collect::<Vec<_>>()` sparingly in `no_std`—that allocation hurts.

Exercise: Optimize a Slow Driver

Write a function that reads 16 bytes from I2C using `write_read`.

Time it using DWT and log the result.

Replace the read with a buffered poll over 8 bytes.

Compare cycle counts and analyze the gain.

If using a `Vec`, replace with a `[u8; 16]` buffer and remeasure.

This will help you connect code structure with performance outcomes directly.

Optimizing embedded Rust firmware is about tightening control over what your code is doing at every level—from cycles to memory to timing behavior. The compiler gives you tools to understand what's really going on. Your job is to measure, observe, and refine until your firmware meets its timing, size, and power goals—consistently, and under real-world conditions.

Chapter 10: Real-World Systems Software Project

Writing drivers, managing memory safely, and interacting with hardware registers are all foundational skills in systems programming—but they aren't the final destination. Real systems work as complete, cohesive utilities. Whether you're building a command-line tool, a logging agent for embedded telemetry, or a tiny TCP-based file server, the real value comes from integrating everything you've learned into something complete, usable, and maintainable.

In this chapter, we're going to walk through the process of building and maintaining a full Rust systems utility. Not a toy or a minimal proof of concept, but a real project with structure, error handling, performance considerations, and deployment-ready reliability. The project we'll use to anchor this chapter is a **custom embedded logger**—a tool that captures serial or networked telemetry from a device, timestamps it, formats it safely, and optionally persists it to a file or forwards it over the network.

Designing and Building a Full System Utility

Writing a complete systems utility isn't just about knowing how to interact with hardware or how to use concurrency. It's about tying everything together into a cohesive program that can run reliably in production, handle errors gracefully, and operate efficiently under real-world constraints. Whether your tool is a custom shell, a telemetry logger, or a lightweight network proxy, the principles are the same: define clear functionality, structure your application for maintainability, and apply the safety and performance principles Rust provides from the ground up.

Define the Purpose and Inputs Clearly

Our tool will:

Read data over a serial port from an embedded device

Timestamp each line using the system clock

Print logs to the screen in real-time

Optionally save logs to a file

Optionally forward them over a TCP connection

Let's start with a minimal CLI skeleton. We'll use `clap` to handle arguments and `tokio` for asynchronous execution.

Add these dependencies to your `Cargo.toml`:

```
[dependencies]

tokio = { version = "1", features = ["full"] }

clap = { version = "4.3", features = ["derive"] }

serialport = "4.2"

chrono = "0.4"

tokio-util = "0.7"
```

Building the CLI Interface

Create a binary with a user-friendly interface:

```rust
use clap::Parser;

#[derive(Parser, Debug)]
#[command(name = "serial-logger")]
#[command(about = "Read logs over UART, timestamp,
and write to stdout or file.")]
struct Args {
    #[arg(short, long, help = "Serial port path,
e.g. /dev/ttyUSB0")]
    port: String,

    #[arg(short, long, help = "Baud rate (default:
115200)")]
    baud: Option<u32>,

    #[arg(short, long, help = "Write logs to this
file path")]
    output: Option<String>,
```

```rust
    #[arg(long, help = "Forward logs to a remote
TCP host")]
    forward: Option<String>,
}

#[tokio::main]
async fn main() -> anyhow::Result<()> {
    let args = Args::parse();
    logger_main(args).await
}
```

Now let's implement `logger_main()` that orchestrates the full task.

Serial Port Setup and Buffered Reader

Rust's `serialport` crate works with `std::io`, but since we're in `tokio`, we'll wrap the stream and adapt it for async reading using `tokio_util::codec::FramedRead`.

```rust
use std::io;
use serialport::SerialPort;
use tokio::io::{AsyncWriteExt};
use tokio::fs::File;
use tokio_util::codec::{FramedRead, LinesCodec};
use chrono::Local;
use std::time::Duration;

async fn logger_main(args: Args) ->
anyhow::Result<()> {
    let baud = args.baud.unwrap_or(115_200);

    let port = serialport::new(&args.port, baud)
        .timeout(Duration::from_millis(100))
        .open()?; // This gives us a Box<dyn
SerialPort>

    let reader =
tokio_serial::SerialStream::new(port);
    let mut lines = FramedRead::new(reader,
LinesCodec::new());

    let mut log_file = match args.output {
```

```
            Some(path) =>
Some(File::create(path).await?),
            None => None,
        };

        while let Some(line) = lines.next_line().await?
{
            let now = Local::now().format("%Y-%m-%d
%H:%M:%S");
            let entry = format!("[{}] {}\n", now,
line);

            print!("{}", entry);

            if let Some(file) = log_file.as_mut() {

file.write_all(entry.as_bytes()).await?;
            }

            if let Some(ref forward_host) =
args.forward {
                send_over_tcp(forward_host,
&entry).await?;
            }
        }

        Ok(())
}
```

Note that we're:

Framing serial input into complete lines

Adding timestamps on the host side

Writing conditionally to file and network

Forwarding Over TCP

If the user provides a --forward host, we'll connect to it and send each log line immediately:

```
use tokio::net::TcpStream;
```

```
async fn send_over_tcp(host: &str, data: &str) ->
anyhow::Result<()> {
    let mut stream =
TcpStream::connect(host).await?;
    stream.write_all(data.as_bytes()).await?;
    Ok(())
}
```

To make this more efficient, you could maintain a persistent connection. But for simplicity and reliability (especially in the face of remote disconnects), we reconnect per message. In production, you might back this with a retry queue and reconnection logic.

Example Run

```
cargo run -- --port /dev/ttyUSB0 --output logs.txt
--forward 192.168.0.100:9000
```

This command:

Connects to /dev/ttyUSB0 at 115200 baud

Reads each line from the serial port

Prepends a timestamp

Prints to stdout

Writes to logs.txt

Sends over TCP to a remote log collector

You now have a fully functional, real-world utility.

Exercise: Add Filtering and Severity Tagging

Extend the logger to support:

Filtering logs with a keyword: --filter error

Detecting severity levels (e.g., lines starting with [ERROR], [WARN], etc.)

Coloring output using ANSI escape codes with the colored crate

161

This will give you practice working with pattern matching, regular expressions, and stream filtering in real time.

Building a full system utility is where all your skills converge:

You handled hardware I/O through a serial interface

You wrote a structured, configurable async task

You added logging and optional file/network integration

You respected safety, performance, and clarity at every step

These same principles scale to tools that live inside embedded environments, host-side automation systems, CI testers, or network daemons. What matters is the discipline: define clear boundaries, isolate concerns, and build from tested, type-safe parts.

This is real systems software—and Rust lets you write it with confidence.

Best Practices for Safety, Concurrency, and Performance

Once your systems utility is structurally complete and functionally correct, the next step is refinement. Writing Rust gives you strong guardrails by default—but you still have to make conscious decisions about **safety**, **concurrency**, and **performance**. These aren't separate concerns—they affect each other constantly. A concurrent routine that isn't safe will crash under pressure. A safe design that's slow won't meet production needs. And performant code that's unsafe won't survive long-term.

In this section, you'll learn how to structure your Rust systems software to maximize **runtime safety**, write **concurrent code that won't race or deadlock**, and **optimize performance** without giving up clarity or maintainability. We'll explore real decisions you face in a project—like how to use `Arc<Mutex<>>` safely, when to prefer channels, how to identify critical paths, and how to structure code that's not only correct but fast and fault-tolerant.

We'll use the logging utility from the last section as our working example and improve it to production-grade quality by applying key best practices.

Enforce Safety Through Types and Ownership

Rust's ownership model already prevents data races and memory unsafety. But you still have to apply that model thoughtfully when designing system-wide coordination.

Take this shared state structure:

```
use std::sync::{Arc, Mutex};

struct LogState {
    count: usize,
    error_count: usize,
}
```

In a concurrent system, you might wrap this in a `Mutex` and share it across threads:

```
let state = Arc::new(Mutex::new(LogState { count:
0, error_count: 0 }));
```

This works, but it's not ideal unless updates to both counters always happen together. If they don't, it's better to split the state:

```
struct LogStats {
    total: AtomicUsize,
    errors: AtomicUsize,
}
```

Now you can update without a lock:

```
use std::sync::atomic::{AtomicUsize, Ordering};

stats.total.fetch_add(1, Ordering::Relaxed);
```

This reduces locking overhead and avoids contention. Always ask: *Is a lock truly necessary?* If you're only updating numeric counters or flags, atomics are usually better.

Avoid long-held locks inside async code.

This is a common anti-pattern:

```
let mut state = shared_state.lock().await;
```

163

```
state.buffer.push(line);
```

If anything inside the locked scope awaits again, it can deadlock. Keep lock scopes small and don't `await` while holding them.

Write Concurrency That Scales Without Conflict

When you're managing multiple producers or consumers—serial readers, file writers, and TCP forwarders—you need a clean handoff mechanism. Channels are ideal for this.

Use `tokio::sync::mpsc` for bounded message passing between tasks:

```
use tokio::sync::mpsc;

let (tx, mut rx) = mpsc::channel::<String>(100);
```

Send from your reader task:

```
tx.send(log_line).await?;
```

Receive in your writer task:

```
while let Some(line) = rx.recv().await {
    file.write_all(line.as_bytes()).await?;
}
```

This decouples reading from writing, and allows backpressure control. If the writer falls behind, the channel fills up and readers will naturally slow down.

Avoid unbounded channels unless you're 100% sure your consumers can keep up.

Make Performance Explicit, Not Accidental

Rust is fast by default—but that doesn't mean all Rust code is fast. You should measure performance directly and write code that behaves predictably under load.

Don't allocate more than necessary.

This:

```
let msg = format!("[{}] {}\n", Local::now(), line);
```

allocates a new string for every log line. That's fine at low rates, but if you're processing thousands of lines per second, use pre-allocated buffers with `heapless::Vec` or reuse `String` with `clear()`.

Avoid unnecessary cloning.

Cloning is cheap for references and primitives, but can be costly for buffers or nested structures.

Instead of this:

```
let copy = log_entry.clone();

queue.push(copy);
```

Pass `Arc<str>` or `Box<str>` if you must share across threads, and avoid deep copies.

Use `#[inline(always)]` judiciously.

Inlining is a performance hint. Use it for short, critical-path functions that are called often:

```
#[inline(always)]

fn crc8(input: &[u8]) -> u8 {

    // fast, small function

}
```

But avoid inlining large functions—you'll just inflate binary size and lose cache efficiency.

Example: Batching File Writes for Efficiency

Let's say you're writing each log line directly to disk. That works, but it's slow. Disk I/O should be buffered.

Batch writes in groups:

```
use tokio::fs::File;
use tokio::io::AsyncWriteExt;
use tokio::time::{timeout, Duration};
```

```rust
use tokio::sync::mpsc;

async fn file_writer(mut rx:
mpsc::Receiver<String>, path: String) ->
anyhow::Result<()> {
    let mut file = File::create(path).await?;
    let mut buffer = Vec::with_capacity(64 * 1024);

    loop {
        match timeout(Duration::from_millis(10),
rx.recv()).await {
            Ok(Some(line)) => {

buffer.extend_from_slice(line.as_bytes());

                if buffer.len() > 32 * 1024 {
                    file.write_all(&buffer).await?;
                    buffer.clear();
                }
            }
            _ => {
                if !buffer.is_empty() {
                    file.write_all(&buffer).await?;
                    buffer.clear();
                }
            }
        }
    }
}
```

Now you're batching small writes into larger ones, reducing system calls and improving throughput dramatically on SSDs and flash storage.

Exercise: Profile and Refactor for Throughput

Take your log reader loop

Add DWT cycle counter instrumentation (on embedded) or wall-clock timing (on host)

Log cycles or milliseconds per batch of 100 lines

Refactor:

Replace per-line I/O with buffered writes

Replace clones with references or `Arc`

Add a bounded channel between producers and consumers

Compare timing before and after. You'll be surprised how much small changes reduce per-line cost.

The best Rust systems code is not just fast or safe in isolation—it's designed to stay fast under pressure, and stay safe when concurrency gets complicated. It's structured, predictable, and measurable.

So remember:

Keep shared state minimal and well-encapsulated

Prefer atomics for counters and flags, not locks

Never `.await` inside a lock scope

Use channels to decouple tasks and avoid race conditions

Batch I/O operations and reuse memory where possible

Rust won't stop you from writing inefficient code—but it gives you all the tools to write software that is simultaneously robust, correct, and fast. Once you internalize these patterns, you'll not only avoid pitfalls—you'll build systems that scale cleanly and fail gracefully under real-world conditions.

Deploying, Auditing, and Maintaining Your Rust Systems Code

Once your Rust systems utility is working well and behaves correctly under stress, the next phase isn't just about finishing development—it's about preparing your software for the real world. That means making it shippable, maintainable, and verifiably secure. You're not just building for yourself anymore. You're building something that needs to run unattended on customer machines, CI environments, or inside production infrastructure.

In this section, we'll walk through how to **deploy**, **audit**, and **maintain** your Rust systems code. We'll make sure that when you release a build, it's small, secure, and traceable. We'll see how to audit your code for unsafe usage and dependency risks, and how to structure your codebase and workflows so updates, patches, and maintenance are straightforward and reliable.

Building for Deployment

The first step to deployment is producing reliable, portable binaries. Rust makes this easy with `cargo build`, but there are a few important steps that turn a basic binary into something that behaves well under real usage.

Always build in release mode:

```
cargo build --release
```

The `--release` flag turns on optimization (`opt-level = 3`) and strips debug symbols by default. But you can fine-tune the release profile for even better results in `Cargo.toml`:

```
[profile.release]
opt-level = "z"
codegen-units = 1
lto = true
strip = true
panic = "abort"
```

`opt-level = "z"` minimizes binary size

`codegen-units = 1` ensures better optimization at link time

`lto = true` enables link-time optimization

`panic = "abort"` avoids stack unwinding code, useful for small binaries

`strip = true` ensures symbols are removed at build time (you can also run `strip` manually)

You'll usually end up with a binary that is 300KB–1MB in size, depending on features.

Cross-Compiling and Static Linking

If you're building for other platforms (e.g., ARM Linux, x86_64 MUSL, or embedded), use cross to handle toolchains and targets:

```
cargo install cross
```

```
cross build --target x86_64-unknown-linux-musl --
release
```

This produces statically linked binaries that work on almost any Linux distro. For embedded systems, choose the appropriate target (e.g., `thumbv7em-none-eabihf`) and set up `.cargo/config.toml` with the right linker and memory.x file.

Dependency and Security Auditing

Once the build is ready, audit it before releasing.

Install **`cargo-audit`**:

```
cargo install cargo-audit
```

Run it:

```
cargo audit
```

This checks your `Cargo.lock` against the RustSec database and alerts you to vulnerabilities in your dependencies.

To enforce audits in CI, add it to your GitHub Actions workflow:

```
- name: Audit dependencies

  run: cargo audit
```

Also use `cargo-deny` to enforce license policies, deny unwanted crates, or restrict duplicate versions:

```
cargo install cargo-deny

cargo deny init

cargo deny check
```

These tools help you maintain a clean, risk-assessed dependency tree—which is critical for any production-facing code.

Managing Unsafe Code

169

Even if your code compiles, you should know where and why you're using `unsafe`.

Use `cargo geiger` to find `unsafe` usage in your code and dependencies:

```
cargo install cargo-geiger

cargo geiger
```

This reports every `unsafe` block and function. If you're building firmware or low-level system utilities, some `unsafe` is expected. But each usage should be minimal, justified, and wrapped in a safe abstraction.

Also, review the safety assumptions you're making in `unsafe` blocks and document them clearly.

Versioning and Releases

Always tag your releases using Git tags that match your crate version:

```
git tag -a v1.0.0 -m "Stable release"

git push origin v1.0.0
```

In `Cargo.toml`, match the crate version:

```
[package]

name = "syslog-bridge"

version = "1.0.0"
```

This helps tooling and CI systems pull the right version and makes issues easier to track.

To publish to crates.io:

```
cargo login

cargo publish
```

To distribute binaries instead, use GitHub Releases or platforms like S3, IPFS, or static hosting.

For self-updating tools, use the `self update` crate to let users fetch the latest binary automatically from GitHub or another endpoint.

Logging, Monitoring, and Runtime Diagnostics

For production utilities, include runtime diagnostics:

Track start time, version, and build hash

Provide CLI flags for verbosity or metrics output

Write logs to file or syslog with `log` and `env_logger` or `tracing`

Example:

```
use log::{info, error};
use env_logger::Env;

fn main() {

env_logger::Builder::from_env(Env::default().defaul
t_filter_or("info")).init();
    info!("System logger starting");
}
```

You can enable this at runtime:

```
RUST_LOG=debug ./syslog-bridge
```

Also consider exporting metrics using Prometheus, `metrics`, or JSON logs for integration into monitoring systems.

Update and Maintenance Strategy

If your utility runs in the field or as part of a larger system, think about:

Configuration: use `toml`, `yaml`, or `clap` with config files

Update channels: stable vs. nightly binaries

Error reporting: structured logs, panic hooks

Long-term support: backporting patches, changelog files

Always include version info in your binary:

```rust
const VERSION: &str = env!("CARGO_PKG_VERSION");

fn print_version() {
    println!("Version: {}", VERSION);
}
```

This helps you trace bug reports back to builds.

Exercise: Harden and Prepare a Binary for Deployment

Add version, license, authors, and description to `Cargo.toml`

Enable `lto`, panic abort, and strip symbols in `[profile.release]`

Use `cross` to build a static Linux binary

Run `cargo audit` and `cargo deny` to ensure no vulnerabilities or license issues

Tag the release with Git and include the changelog

Upload the binary to GitHub or your distribution channel

This gives you a complete pipeline from clean code to traceable, deployable output.

Building great systems code is only the beginning. What makes it usable and trusted is your attention to how it's **built**, how it's **inspected**, and how it's **maintained**. Rust helps you here not just by compiling your code but by giving you a healthy ecosystem of tooling to reason about its safety, performance, and reliability.

Appendix

A: Rust Tooling and Build System (Cargo)

Rust's build and package management system is called **Cargo**. It's more than just a build tool—it handles compilation, dependency resolution, testing, benchmarking, documentation generation, and publishing. Every Rust project is organized around a `Cargo.toml` file, which defines the project's metadata, dependencies, and configuration.

A basic project structure looks like this:

```
my_project/
├── Cargo.toml
└── src/
    └── main.rs
```

To create a new project:

```
cargo new my_project
```

This initializes a Git repository with a minimal Rust project.

To build your project:

```
cargo build
```

For a release-optimized build:

```
cargo build --release
```

To run the application:

```
cargo run
```

To test:

```
cargo test
```

To document:

```
cargo doc --open
```

Cargo manages dependencies via the `Cargo.toml` file. Add a dependency like so:

```
[dependencies]

tokio = { version = "1", features = ["full"] }
```

Then run `cargo build` again, and Cargo will fetch and compile the dependency.

Cargo supports **workspace** projects, allowing multiple crates in one repository. You can define a `Cargo.toml` at the root level with:

```
[workspace]
members = ["libcore", "firmware", "cli"]
```

This is helpful for organizing larger projects into logical parts—like a library, a CLI frontend, and a backend service.

Appendix B: Unsafe Rust Patterns and Guidelines

Rust's safety guarantees rely on its strict compile-time checks. However, there are situations—especially in systems programming—where you need to bypass those checks to work directly with memory, raw pointers, or foreign interfaces. That's where the `unsafe` keyword comes in.

Declaring something `unsafe` doesn't mean the code is automatically dangerous. It means **you are taking responsibility** for upholding Rust's safety guarantees manually.

Common patterns where `unsafe` is required:

Dereferencing raw pointers (`*const T`, `*mut T`)

Calling functions from C (`extern "C" fn`)

Accessing hardware registers (memory-mapped I/O)

Implementing `unsafe` traits like `Send` or `Sync`

Manual memory allocation and deallocation

Example of reading from a raw pointer:

```
let ptr: *const u32 = 0x4000_0000 as *const u32;
let val: u32 = unsafe {
core::ptr::read_volatile(ptr) };
```

Key guidelines when using `unsafe`:

Keep unsafe code in isolated functions or modules

Document all safety assumptions clearly

Wrap unsafe operations in safe abstractions

Never call `unsafe` code unless you fully understand its invariants

Run tools like `cargo-geiger` to audit usage

Unsafe code should be rare, deliberate, and surrounded by tests. If you find yourself writing a lot of unsafe code, pause and reconsider the architecture. Often, a safer pattern is available with slightly more abstraction.

Appendix C: Useful Crates for Systems Development

The Rust ecosystem includes many crates that are particularly useful when building low-level systems utilities, firmware, or performance-critical tools.

Here are some widely adopted and well-maintained crates you'll likely use:

tokio – Asynchronous runtime for networking, I/O, and concurrency

async-std – Alternative async runtime with a standard library feel

serialport – Cross-platform serial port access

clap / **structopt** – CLI argument parsing

tracing – Structured logging for async-aware applications

log + **env_logger** – Simple logging mechanism with filtering

heapless – Data structures for `no_std` systems without dynamic memory

embedded-hal – Common traits for embedded peripherals (I2C, SPI, GPIO, etc.)

`defmt` – Low-overhead logging for embedded targets

`anyhow` / `thiserror` – Simplify error handling with backtraces and context

`criterion` – Statistical benchmarking for performance testing

`cross` – Build and test for multiple targets (e.g., ARM, x86_64-musl)

`cargo-audit` – Scan dependencies for vulnerabilities

`cargo-deny` – Enforce license and dependency policies

All of these crates are maintained by active communities, and many are supported by working groups inside the Rust project or companies that deploy Rust in production systems.

Appendix D: Further Learning and Community Resources

If you're continuing your work in systems programming with Rust, there are excellent resources to expand your understanding and connect with other developers.

Books and References:

The Rust Programming Language – Official and comprehensive Rust guide

Rust for Rustaceans by Jon Gjengset – In-depth topics for experienced Rust developers

The Embedded Rust Book – Beginner-to-intermediate resource for `no_std` development

Rust Atomics and Locks by Mara Bos – Deep understanding of concurrency primitives

Online Resources:

rust-lang.org – Official site for docs, downloads, and guides

docs.rs – Documentation for every crate on crates.io

lib.rs – Alternative crate search with scoring and maintenance info

areweasyncyet.rs – Guide to async Rust

ferrous-systems.com – Training, tools, and blog content for embedded Rust

Community and Discussion:

users.rust-lang.org – Official user forum

Zulip Chat – Technical conversations for the Rust project

Reddit – Discussions, questions, and news

Rust Discord – Real-time chat with thousands of Rust users

Contribution Opportunities:

Look for issues labeled `E-easy` or `good first issue` on GitHub

Join the Embedded WG, Async WG, or specific crate working groups

Contribute to open-source drivers, HALs, or Rust-based operating system components

By staying connected to the ecosystem and continuously refining your knowledge, you not only grow your technical capabilities—you also help build and support the ongoing success of Rust in systems-level development. Whether you're writing firmware, building automation tools, or architecting production infrastructure, Rust has the tooling, community, and power to support you.